Impact of Integrated Rural Development Programmes

Impact of Integrated Rural Development Programmes

S.U. Dar

ANMOL PUBLICATIONS PVT. LTD.
NEW DELHI - 110 002 (INDIA)

ANMOL PUBLICATIONS PVT. LTD.
H.O.: 4374/4B, Ansari Road, Darya Ganj,
New Delhi-110 002 (India)
Ph.: 23278000, 23261597
B.O.: No. 1015, Ist Main Road, BSK IIIrd Stage
IIIrd Phase, IIIrd Block,
Bangalore - 560 085 (India)
Visit us at: www.anmolpublications.com

Impact of Integrated Rural Development Programmes

First Published, 2007

ISBN 81-7041-601-9

PRINTED IN INDIA

Printed at Mehra Offset Press, Delhi.

Preface

Village in our country is an important social and economic unit in Indian society. However, rural development is broader concept and is concerned with the total development of rural economy which covers the maximum area and maximum people. In other words it is comprehensive and multi dimensional concept and encompasses the development of all sectors in rural areas. As a concept it connotes overall development of rural areas with a view to improve the quality of life of rural people.

After independence various development efforts have been initiated by the Government of India and State Government. Now this process is diverted towards rural sector as rural development is not only the result of efforts made through economic planning and resource allocation for the sector but also depends upon the positive response of various determinant factors operating in the rural economy. These factors are both economic and non-economic which determine the shape, level and direction of rural development. The present book covers diverse aspects of the subject through various papers.

The first paper of the book by Dr. Mittal and Dr. Kumar aims at comprehending the theme, concepts, approaches and strategies of rural development. The paper on decentralisation perspective by Awasthi emphasized that the prerequisite of successful decentralised planning is to create a proper environment—to bring a kind of attitudinal change among the poor people towards various developmental activities.Their role ought not be merely to formulate and implement programmes but also to ensure that the benefits of these development efforts are made available to the poor people. In order to meet the problem of growing unemployment, India needs an employment policy. It was, therefore, felt necessary in the different plants to have supplemental programmes for specific target groups/ areas for employment creation, income generation and poverty alleviation. All these issues are discussed in a paper by Dr. Mittal and Dr. Kumar in the context of rural development.

Since last two decades the twin problems of Manpower Planning i.e., 'Poverty' ,and 'Unemployment' have drawn a great deal of attention of the intellectuals, planners, and policy makers in Inida, the different Government agencies as well as the individual scholars are at a loss to know as how to pinpoint the hard care of poor and unemployed in a vast country where diversity prevails from natural, social and economic fronts and the planners and policy-makers are unable to understand as to how it should be attacked. As a result, in many parts of India, dedicated and very successful experiments are being made for finding new ways of alleviating poverty and unemployment. It is discussed by Rajendra P. Mamgain in his paper entitled 'Poverty, Unemployment and Manpower Planning.'

N. Sridharan's paper on democratic planning highlights that the slogan 'Garibi Hatao' is included in all the plan but still the problem of poverty is acute. The paper draws the attention that there is lack of coordination between different developmental programmes and implementing agencies and the planning process is much influenced by politicians. He also criticises the functioning of IRD programmes which are of short nature and suggests some long-term measure for the removal of poverty and unemployment. Today need of hour is the proper planning and development of human resources of balanced development.

Dr. Dubey's paper starts with two basic promises. First, in analysis of regional disparities units of investigation should be as homogenious as possible and practicable and adopted district as unit of investigation which has been acclaimed as most effective unit to represent the grassroots realities. Secondly, it is limited to demographic development. It takes a comprehensive view of demographic development. In consonant with the basic premise remaining part of the paper is organised in order of a conceptual, analytical and synthesis sequence. Finally, he concluded that southern India is relatively at higher demographic development plan than the north India. In other words the most part of the country has attained the state where physical factors in the determination of demographic performance of the area are relatively less significant than the socio-economic and cultural factors. In the last he suggsted some policy options.

Dr. Kumar in his paper Roaming around the poverty has highlighted the issues and need of basic infrastructure for rural development in BIMARU states. He has suggested that unless basic infrastructure is provided like, irrigation, electricity, communication etc. all the efforts being made for rural development will not yield the fruitful result.

Various programmes and policies have been launched by the Government of India for removal of rural unemployment and the Jawahar Rozgar Yojna is one of them. In a paper Dr. Mittal and Dr. Kumar has stated that JRY basically has nothing new to offer. It is simply a case of merging partially successful schemes into one and re-christening it to raks the populationalism. The programme shall run into the problems of not being able to satisfy the objective of employment generation in terms of the number of workers employed, owing to the constraints of minimum wages, total funds at its disposal, minimum number of days for which employment has to be provided and fixed cost of materials.

Pradhan and Mamgain have reached to the conclusion that IRDP—despite all its shortcomings, provide assistance to the rural poor irrespective of whether they are farmers or artisans or craftsman. Though the earlier programme viz. SFDA might have helped in the upliftment of small farmers but obviously its impact on rural disparities has been marginal. Another paper by K.M. George also throw light on the importance of IRDP programme. How IRDP can become more relevant has been discussed in detail in the paper.

An empirical investigation of Dr. Shobhan Singh Khanka on the problems of Entrepreneurship Development in Kumaun, U.P. has stated that the enterprising attitude has been no more an acumen which one gets from his very birth, but it is the acumen that can be inculcated by imparting education and training to the prospective people. Further, he argued that entrepreneurship is a set of attributes which the entrepreneurs possess and which help them be have entrepreneurially. Another important aspect of rural area is industrialisation on which a base study is done by Dr. Singh. He suggests that the industrial development in rural area would have certainly included three major consequences i.e. (a) management of traditional village artisans; (b) development of major agro-industry like sugar, and (c) development of small scale village and cottage industries. These schemes should preferably be small labour intensive technologies because of the unskilled labour in rural areas and scarce foreign exchange in India.

Women and their problems have acquired a steadily growing importance in social research. It is in this view the paper 'Female Labour Participation in Household and Non-household Industry' by Dr. Kumar seeks to examine the trends in sex ratio, educational structure and the trends of female labour force participation in rural and urban areas of India. The focus is primarily on household and non-household industry occupations and investigated with two digit Indian Standard Industrial Classification (ISIC).The extent of females participation relative to males in household and non-household industry has also been studied. Finally paper concludes that women participate in limited number of industries which are characterised by high labour intensity and tediousness less mobility, less skill, coupled with less remuneration.

Dr. Mittal in her paper 'Women's Participation in Rural Local Level Institutions' highlighted that women's participation in the Panchayati Raj is not upto the mark. Mere reservation will not solve the problem unless women members are given commensurate powers to function effectively.

Last paper of the book i.e. 'Rural Development has miles to go' Dr. Gupta and editor Dr. Mittal has concluded that complex nature of the development in the rural areas demand a multi-disciplinary, multi-sectoral and multi-agency approach to rural development planning.

I acknowledge with a sense of deep gratitude to all the contributions who were kind enough to prepare well researched articles on the requested themes. Their enthusiastic response was great stimulus for the preparation of this volume.

I owe a special debt to Dr. Sunit Gupta who was not always encourage me but as active partner in planning and execution of the study. Dr. Gupta helped me a lot in getting the manuscript ready in publishable form. My sincere thanks are also due to Shri S.A. Khan Regional Director, NIPCCD Regional Centre, Lucknow.

My thanks are also to the distinguished contributors of this volume and all my colleagues and friends who helped me in someway or the other.

List of Contributors

1. Dr. Ashok Kumar
   Faculty Member
   NIPCCD Regional Centre
   Kursi Road, Gudamba
   Lucknow.

2. Dr. I.C. Awasthi
   Faculty Member
   Institute of Applied Manpower Research
   I.P. Estate, Ring Road
   New Delhi-110 002.

3. Dr. K.M. George
   Director
   CRATPAW
   New Delhi.

4. Dr. K.N. Dubey
   Reader
   Deptt. of Geography
   Lucknow University
   Lucknow.

5. Dr. Mukta Mittal
   NIPCCD Regional Centre
   Kursi Road, Gudamba
   Lucknow.

6. Dr. M. Shridhran
   Director Special Project
   CRATPAW
   New Delhi.

7. Dr. P.C. Pradhan
   Personal Executive
   NALCO, Angul, Dhenkanal
   Orissa

8. Dr. R.P. Mamgain
   Faculty Member
   Institute of Applied Manpower Research
   I.P. Estate, Ring Road
   New Delhi-110 002.

9. Dr. R.B. Singh
   Deptt. of Geography
   University of Delhi
   Delhi.

10. Dr. Sobhan Singh Khanka
    Associate Professor
    IGNOU, New Delhi.

11. Dr. Sunit Gupta
    Director
    Institute for Environmental Development Studies
    Husaingunj
    Lucknow.

Contents

1
Rural Development in India: Retrospect and Prospect

MUKTA MITTAL AND ASHOK KUMAR

Introduction

There has been considerable discussion of the need for and the nature of shifts in emphasis and approach called for in rural development in keeping with the objective of overall development policy for speedy alleviation of poverty. However, one may identify a few factors in common without wishing to over-simplify or over-generalise issues of policy and problems of implementation which are by no means uniform from country to country'.

— that development approaches tended to over-play 'quantity' and speed at the expense of 'equality' and speed at the expense of 'equality and composition';
— that the resources that were in fact committed to rural development were applied unevenly, that they were appropriated in undue proportion for the benefit of an elitist minority;
— that models of development used, explicitly or implicitly, by planners, were urban/industry biased, resulting in a neglect of or at least in inadequate attention to the imperatives of rural development;
— that the bulk of the programme tended to be formulated and implemented from above, with little real role for the rural majority in this process.

However, Rural Development has been in and out of focus of political decision-making many times, but again it is 'in'— and this time it is expected to be integrated. Rural development is an elastic concept and everyone interprets it in his own way. About half-a-century back Gandhiji said 'India lives in villages' but this is true of today too. As per 1981 census, nearly 77 per cent of total population lives in the rural areas comprising 5.76 lakh villages. The idea of village self-sufficiency has recently received great deal of attention from social scientists and policy-makers. The reasons for this may be political, academic or even human considerations. In fact, the problem of improving the lot of seventy per cent of our population that lives in rural areas has assumed greater significance because of its explosive nature which is threatening our very existence. Vast number of people in rural areas live below the poverty line. They include landless labourers, small farmers, artisans and other weaker sections of society. They have been subjected to economic deprivation, discrimination and oppression of the worst kind and of all types. Their abject poverty and sub-human living conditions were standing monuments and living expressions that demanded a new policy framework which gave priority to the amelioration of the lot of our village population[2]. Improving the quality of life of these people became the subject of national and international debates.

'Development of rural areas has been one of the abiding concerns in the various five year plans. The gains of various programmes primarily accrued to the upper strata of rural society. Hence, the government has committed to the philosophy of social justice and socio-economic development of the rural areas. The Government of India started its plan of planned growth soon after independence. These plans had very clear and specific objectives to achieve, namely, eradication of poverty and reducing disparities both between the urban and rural sector and within each sector itself. Thus, the villages were to be provided with modern amenities and their standard of living was to be raised, so as to reduce the disparities between urban and rural sector. At the same time a programme of action was to be launched coupled with massive propaganda and economic incentives to reduce the disparities between the 'haves' and 'havenots' in the rural sector itself and elimination of privileges of chosen few.

Rural Development as a concept is not a new one. It had received the attention of people like Gandhiji, Tagore and many others much before independence. Tagore's Shantiniketan was perhaps the first systematic attempt in this direction. The problem of rural reconstruction however was concretised by Gandhiji. He experienced the toil, drudgery and sub-human living conditions in villages of India. Having lived it, Gandhiji knew for certain that unless and until the village economy of India, he said with agony and anguish lives in villages and India's salvation lay in rural reconstruction. It is not surprising, thus, to note that the new government decided to give highest priority to agriculture and rural development programmes. The driving force behind such a philosophy were a firm belief in the humanities ideology of Gandhiji and a very rational approach of increasing agricultural productivity.

The idea of integrated rural development is the result of our experiences gained through various programmes designed for rural development. Even as a concept our thinking on rural reconstruction has undergone a lot of changes. Rural development earlier was taken to be synonymous with agricultural development. The significance of agriculture development cannot be underscored. It is not only basic for the development of rural areas but also of the industrial sector as it supplies the major and necessary raw material for many industries. The rural sector is expected to provide the necessary savings for investment in industrial economy. It was soon realised that rural development was much broader in its scope. It meant developing the necessary infrastructure cottage and small industries as well as secondary and tertiary sectors such as marketing which are vital for the process of economic development.

Rural development strategies by force of circumstances have been dynamic in nature. Community development and national extension blocks were started in the early fifties as a part of rural reconstruction programme. The panacea for rural problems was seen, at that time, through the development of agriculture and allied sector. The CDP did have its impact on the socio-cultural mores of the rural people and created a wiol in the village masses to improve their lot. Community development may have not achieved much, but its role cannot be minimised. If nothing else they generated hope in the rural masses. However, CDP could not achieve anything remarkable in the agricultural economy of our country. Ford Foundation Committee report in 1959 on 'India's Food Crisis' suggested intensive agricultural work in certain selected areas with perennial irrigation facilities. It also recommended that the government of India should start emergency food production schemes, as well, on a war footing. The Committee gave detailed estimates of ndia's growing food requirements for its overgrowing population. It stressed setting up of separate organisation, staffed by experts and able administrators who could meet the challenge of producing enough food for its teeming millions.

The government of India accepted its recommendations in toto and set up the Intensive Agricultural District Programmes in certain selected districts all over the country. A Central Organisation with the District Collector as its head was set up for achieving higher productivity in food. The Collector was made responsible for coordinating the work of the various functional experts who were responsible for marketing, storage, irrigation, purchases, cooperatives and demonstration activities of the agency. The experiments were a definite success inasmuch as the farmers readily adopted the scientific farming techniques.

An evolution of the IADP programme however revealed certain lacunae which created the base for an intensive development plan. It was felt that IADP was not the answer to the problem of rural development. It just touched the periphery of the problem. Agricultural development was just one part of the total development process. There were many other developmental sectors ancillary to agriculture which could not be touched in the IADP programme. Besides this, the administrative boundaries of the district were hard obstacles to scientific development and optimal utilisation of irrigation, land, human and energy resources.

The Integrated Rural Development Plan was conceived as a result of our experience in the IADP and the insights so gained. A task force was set up by the Planning Commission in 1971 to examine a proposal for Integrated Rural Development and prepare a blue print of such a plan for approval of the appropriate authorities. The task force submitted its first report on Integrated Agricultural Development Projects in 1972.

The recommendations of the task force regarding IRDP (Integrated Rural Development Plan) were accepted by the government. A committee of experts under the guidance of the Minister for Agriculture was set up to give final shape to the recommendations of the task force of rural development. A major feature of the IRDP is its emphasis that development to be successful shall have to be by the people, of the people and for the people. As such people's participation in IRDP is a prior condition for its success. Another a prior factor for the success of the plan, it was conceived, was the judicious application of science and technology for optimum utilisation of resources. The plan emphasised that if it was to be a success it must have a strong organisational base, staffed by experienced personnel and experts who should not only be able to coordinate the various functional activities, but should come out of their ivory towards and seek people's participation. It, thus, emphasised the role of socio-political influences of experts, officials and the people both in the planning and implementation of IRDP programmes.

Let us now examine the basic elements of the rural scenario. It is necessary to identify these to give directionality to our developmental efforts. These may be briefly summed up as:

(a) Natural resources management such as land, water, management, fisheries, poultry, dairy farming, etc.

(b) Exploiting natural resources for human welfare would include utilisation of existing energy resources effectively and developing new sources of energy.

(c) Managing human skills and developing, it would include identifying craftsmen engaged in cottage and small industries which could be run through local skills, providing training and management and marketing of the village industrial produce.

(d) Maintenance systems would include health and family welfare and improving the living conditions and a better quality life.

(e) Development system would include education and cultural activities.

(f) Humanistic systems refer to social welfare programmes for weaker sections of society (including women and children), ameliorating the lot of poorer section of society etc.

It may thus be said, that agricultural development is a major part of rural development but that is not the total plan. Rural development of the rural economy as a whole. Rural development is a wholistic concept rather than a sequential one. Thus, it is equally concerned with the development of infrastructure like roads, transport, power, insurance and banking, development of cottage industries, rural poverty, unemployment, encouraging traditional crafts and industries and providing modern education, health facilities and providing cheap but decent houses for the rural poor and deprived.

An integrated development plan has to be based upon the concept of 'self-help' and will, thus, be in consonance with grassroot resources and on intimate knowledge of local needs and indigenous solutions mainly.

It would be interesting to examine the rural scenario at macro-level before making a micro-analysis which we propose to do as a result of our empirical study. Experts have, thus, suggested introduction of mixed farming for small and marginal farmers. Dairy animals are his best form of security financially as well as from the point of view of his health. Dairy animals provide him with best form of protein. However, it has along gestation period, requires huge investments and the task of maintaining these animals is also back-breaking as such small and marginal farmers hardly go in for specialised dairy farming and are content with producing cattle fodder mainly.

However, the role of animal husbandry cannot be emphasised. The 'operation flood' has been a success beyond all over imaginations. The Amul project in district Kaira in Gujarat State is a cooperative with a membership of a 2.5 lakh families and distributes milk and milk products valued around Rupees thirty crores annually. Even though it may not be possible to advocate specialised dairy farming for the small and marginal farmer, some changes ought to be introduced in the cropping pattern so that along with the usual grain and cash crops they can utilize straw, agricultural activities.

If the standard of living has to be raised of these poor farmers from that of abject poverty and despair, they should be encouraged to take to poultry farming, piggery and fishery. In certain parts of the country, maximisation of land use could be a reality if fisheries could be mixed with duck rearing. However, now it is felt that the IRD programme has helped a large number of households to move above the poverty line. There has been a significant decline in the percentage of population living below the poverty line — it declined from 48.3 per cent in 1977-78 to 37.4 per cent in 1983-84 for the country as a whole. For the rural sector it declines from 51.2 per cent to 40.4 per cent during the corresponding period. There are as many as 272 million persons in the country who still groan under poverty, but the bulk i.e. 81 per cent of whom live in the rural sector. The benefits of economic development have yet to fully percolate to this vulnerable section of the society. The IRD programme owns its origin to the consistent thinking of the planners. The sixth plan indicted that though a number of programmes had been in operation for the development of the rural poor, significant improvement could not be achieved among the poorest people in rural areas. These programmes did not cover the whole country, though a large number of blocks in the country had more than one of these programmes operating simultaneously in the same area and for the same target groups. This territorial overlap combined with different funding patterns of these programmes, not only created considerable difficulties in effective monitoring and accounting but also blurred the programme objectives. It was, therefore, proposed that such multiplicity of agencies should be ended and replaced by the single integrated programme called IRDP, operative throughout the country.

Thus, IRDP is to be seen as an instrument for eradicating poverty in the rural sector. The programme of asset endowment under IRDP is designed to develop self-employment ventures in a variety of activities like agriculture, animal husbandry sector, and service and business activities in the tertiary sector.

Why Rural Development?

Rural development, according to the World Bank, 'is a strategy designed to improve the economic and social life of a specific group of people — the rural poor. It involves extending the benefits of development to the poorest among those who seek a livelihood in the rural areas. The group includes small scale farmers, tenants and the landless'. (World Bank, 1975). The World Bank and other international agencies and institutions did place the main emphasis on increasing production, raising productivity, increasing employment and mobilizing what land, labour and capital were available.

Modern development policy-makers, while recognizing the importance of infrastructure, have been ambiguous about the contents of infrastructure. Infrastructure included all things provided by the government which promote directly or indirectly productive activities. Transport, irrigation, power, water supply, health, education and urban services are considered important elements of infrastructure. In a mixed economy with a relatively important public sector, provision of infrastructure has to be carefully planned and provided by the government. Most social and economic indicators such as life expectancy, income, physical infrastructure, social services and literacy consistently show that rural areas compare unfavourably with urban areas (Lipton, 1977). Partly it is the result of avowed change of emphasis in the policy of international institutions like the World Bank. The Bank has recently popularized the problem of rural poverty and the concept of rural development and encouraged its introduction into the official development plan documents of almost all developing countries which are members of the World Bank. Other international agencies like the Food and Agriculture Organisation (FAO), the International Labour Office of the United Nations and other agencies, have also highlighted the need for rural development. However, although the words are spoken and written, emphasies change with time and the fashionable rhetoric cannot always be translated into action because of the needs to satisfy tenders, donors and governments and to ensure some sort of return of investment. However, the need for a new emphasis on rural development becomes clear in the 1970s for four main reasons[3] :

First, about two-thirds of the population of developing countries live in rural areas and there is a higher proportion of rural dwellers in the poorer countries. The rate of growth of these populations has also increased in recent years. The number and proportions of poor people in the rural areas are variously estimated at 750-1000 million people, consisting approximately 33.50 per cent of the rural population in developing countries. If these people are to have raised 'levels of life sustenance, human dignity and freedom' when there is an absence of any rapid expansion in the urban and industrial sectors, income and employment opportunities have to be generated in rural areas to exploit labour, to generate development, and to health rural-urban migration.

Second, the accelerated population growth had helped create serious social and economic problems. Perhaps the most important of these has been a somewhat unexpected and pronounçed increase in open unemployment and underemployment. This is more pronounced in land and resource-scarce situations where the proportion of underemployed rural landless labourers has been increasing. The International Labour Office (ILO), in recognition of these symptoms carried out a number of research studies around the globe as a part of their world employment programme.

Third, despite substantial and impressive increases in growth of agricultural and food output in some regions of a number of developing countries, the plight of the landless labourers and small farmers has not been improved significantly. This is mainly because the increases output productivity have been achieved by provision and use of yield-raising inputs and technology by those with the ability, information and political power to demand these things. Thus, unavoidably, in the absence of any significant land reform, poverty for those without land is intimately related to the concentration of land in the hands of large farmers and land owners. These producers can achieve higher yields and output through greater use of machines and other inputs rather than by significantly increasing the use of local labour. The responsibility for this socially inappropriate agricultural growth lies with the international aid-donors and the national development strategies. Recent shifts in the attitudes of aid agencies and the national development policy-makers, at least in their writings, is a recognition of the plight of landless labourers and marginal farmers who did not get a share in the fruits of recent growth of output.

Finally, the success of some of the developing countries in eliminating destitution and unemployment through a system of communes attracted the attention (and sometimes the concern) of policy-makers around the world. Government and international agencies started a search for alternatives to collectivist models; this led to many 'reformist' experiments in rural development.

The Concept of Integrated Rural Development

There are many different types and meanings of 'integrated rural development' and what is 'integrated' depends more on the writer than anything else. As Lea (1980) points out, there are some semantic difficulties. Its integration means seeing things as a whole or completing something by combining parts into a whole, and if development is something which can be 'assessed properly only in terms of the total human needs, values and standards of the good life and the good society perceived by the very societies undergoing change' adding 'integrated' to 'development' is tautological. Also it is hard to imagine effective farm of rural planning that does not seek to develop urban places and integrate them effectively, in a non-exploitative way, into the rural scheme of things.

The idea of integrated rural is not particularly new. Mahatma Gandhi and Mao Zedony, who differed radically in both philosophy as well as strategy, shared a common vision of rural development. Both leaders felt the need for ensuring that the masses had adequate employment so that their basic minimum needs in food, clothing, shelter, education and health care were met. Both stressed the role of mass participation and involvement and the need for the leadership to identify with the masses. Mahatma Gandhi writing in 1920 says:

Every village's first concern will be to grow its own crops and cotton for its cloth. It should have a reserve for its cattle, recreation and playgrounds for adult and children. Then if there is more land available it will grow useful money crops. This will maintain a village, therefore, school and public hall. It will have its own water-works ensuring clean supply. This can be done through controlled wells and tanks. Education will be compulsory up to the final basis. there will be no castes as we have today, with their graded un-touchability. Non-violence with its technique of 'Satyagraha' and non-cooperation will be the sanction of the village community. There will be a compulsory service of village grands who will be selected by rotation from the register, maintained by the village. The government of the village will be conducted by the 'Panchayat' of five persons, annually elected by the adult villagers, male and female, possessing minimum prescribed qualifications. These will have all the authority and jurisdiction required. Since there will be no system of punishments in the accepted sense, this 'Panchayat' will be the legislature, judiciary, executive combined to operate for its years of office.

Integrated rural development of Mao's and Mahatma Gandhi's conception is an organic integration while a western-trained social scientist tends to see it in terms of provision of inputs and infrastructure required to raise outputs and productivity. This become apparent after the Second World War. The post-war development strategy was aimed at industrialization and was a copy of the western historical experience of economic development.

While dealing with approach, strategy and perspective of integrated rural development, Sharma and Malhotra defined Integrated Rural Development as follows: 'It is a synergistic approach aiming at total development of the area and the people by bringing about the necessary institutional attitudinal changes and by delivering a package of services through extension methods to encompass not only to economic field, i.e. development of agriculture, rural industries act, but also the establishment of the required special infrastructure and services in the area of health and nutrition, education and literacy, basic civic amenities, family planning etc. with an ultimate objective of improving quality of life in the rural areas.

While expressing the views on some aspects of rural development

Mishra and Sundaram conceived it as a desired positive change in the rural areas — both in a quantitative as well as a qualitative sense. Thus, rural development is an area concept. It is completed term which integrates a variety of human life and activities which can broadly be classified into the broad dimensions of social, economic, technological and natural rural development means desired changes in all these dimensions.

However, in brief it can be stated that 'Rural development involves a complex process of change in rural sub-systems and their interaction, leading to desired improvements in rural income employment opportunities, incomes distribution, rural welfare and other aspects of rural life'. An integrated rural development programmes, therefore, is viewed as 'a package of action which covers a series of mutually supporting projects and activities concerned with different sectors of rural communities'.

Planning for Integrated Rural Development

An ideally formulated workable and consistent rural development plan would have many facets and be 'optimally balanced'. Optimal balance implies that different goals and targets, in addition to being feasible and mutually supportive, should be achievable with minimum input of effort and resources, ensuring efficiency and economy of resource use.

Planning for rural development is a long-term on-going process with goals, long run plans and time-bound specific plans with targets dovetailing one another. Local grassroot participation in this process is essential. Such a process is feasible if there is pressure for its success from above and below. Enlightened national leadership can and does provide this pressure from above, while grassroot local peasant and rural workers organisation can also provide this pressure from below. Thus, planning for rural development in this sense is rather sophisticated business and the role of the government in initiating and implementing programmes is crucial.

Despite some differences, the following important characteristics seem common to most developing countries and have a bearing on their approach to rural development.

(i) Agriculture has been a way of life for a majority of the people for at least 5000-6000 years and the organization of rural society is complex, structured and based on a patronage-clientele principle. Basically it is a capitalist system of agriculture with feudalist overtones.

(ii) Foreign colonial rule for 100-150 years in most of the developing countries gave rise to 'economic dualism' through the introduction of commercial crops, large-scale mining and plantations. The structural rigidities of the latter retarded transformation and induced a process of underdevelopment. While it is true there is plenty of overlap and interconnectivity between the peasant and commercial systems, the viciousness of dualism lies in the fact that the commercial sector sees itself as superior and does little help to peasant or subsistence sector. In most ways is exploits the peasants and works against equalization.

(iii) British and foreign rulers interfered with the land-tenure systems and left a legacy of a class of intermediaries who are 'parasites' or a 'rent collecting class' in economic terms.

(iv) Government of these countries immediately after independence in the late 1940s and early 1950s set about the task of reforming the land tenure system with rather limited success.

(v) Every state in the Third World has a centralised planning body which formulated development plans for hierarchical and authoritarian administration. This approach is now being termed a 'top-down' approach. Rural development ought to come to terms with these plans, but it does not. References to rural development in the plan documents are incidental to the agricultural sector infrastructure development.

However, all too often data collection and plan-writing can so easily become exercises in themselves, remote from problems of implementation and management. Chambers (1974, 32 ff) sees managed procedures as the key to effective rural development and plan formulation as only one part in a set of six clusters of procedures which continuously affect to modify each other.

In all the above six links, local participation seems central to rural development planning. It is central because the local people are the main actors in the drama and the other five links are necessary enabling conditions. Target-setting and plan formulation even with the best of research support and field staff will not lead to the integrated rural development of the type described above. Local participation in rural development effort through local decision-making and local institutions has been emphasised by all nationalist social reformers interested in rural development. We have already referred to the views of Gandhi and Mao in this context. Methods and institutional arrangements involving the local rural communities differs radically in different socio-economic systems. In a collective system of Mao's conception ideology and party play a dominant role, while the Gandhian approach emphasises self-government and spontaneous and voluntary effort induced by local and rural leadership. Regional development planning and decentralization of decision-making can be some of the means of achieving participatory rural development.

It is in this context what we really mean by rural development planning in most countries in a series of 'project' and 'programmes' for rural areas which are either identified and initiated by benevolent donor countries. Researchers in this field, if they take their profession seriously, will find that the information they need is not what they can obtain. Therefore, their only positive role is to raise the right questions and try to understand the working of the rural systems of these countries. Their acquired knowledge will be useful when the policy-making are ready for real rural development planning.

Rural Development during Pre- and Postindependence India

Pre-Independence: Rural development traces back its history to the seventeenth century when voluntary efforts to serve the mankind were initiated. A religious society of people known as 'Friends' or 'Quakers' had emerged as a movement in this direction for the first time in England, then the other parts of the world in rapid strides. It aimed at providing service to mankind transcending bonds of religion, territory and culture. The Quakers was a kind of rebel. In the mid of the seventeeth century, the main plan of the Quaker movement was that every human being has infinite dignity, that he is worthy of reverence simply because he is a human being and therefore a temple of God'. The main spirit behind this movement has been one of the selfless sacrifice and it runs like a wire, as it were among the exponents of the Quaker faith.

However, the first attempt for rural development in India was made in 1885 with an ultimate objective of bringing immediate relief and development of rural areas in Baroda[5]. In 1992, the **Swaraj Ashram** was established at Baroda by Magan Lal Gandhi. The Ashram aimed at preparing for non-cooperation, and the civil disobedience movement launched by the Indian National Congress under the leadership of Gandhi.

With the start of the reform movement by Adivasis during the period 1915-1920, the government suffered heavy losses in revenue, sales of liquor and contractors reduced drastically and the **Adivasis** also refused to do the agricultural work on low wages[6]. In 1935, reconstruction centres were organised at several places, but start of the Second World War in September 1939 thwarted the progress of achievements of these centres.

'Gros more food' campaign was started in 1943 with a view to augmenting the level of food production through planning and implementation of short-term and long-term improvement programmes in agriculture[7]. Besides, a good number of projects at community development were introduced in different parts of country. The next important step was taken by the **Kisan Sabha** under the leadership of the Communist Party Worker, Mrs. Godavari Parulekar in 1945[8]. For the first time, **Adivasis** made slogans against exploitation by landlords, moneylenders and contractors. As a result, the Minimum Wages Act was brought under enforcement in forties to safeguard the interest of Adivasis working for forest contractors. And since 1947, the Government started to encourage formation of Cooperative Labour Contract Societies for forest workers.

However, since start of the last decade of the nineteenth century, quite a few centres of rural reconstruction were started from time to time in different parts of the country. These centres made systematic efforts for development of life and society of specific rural communities and tried to make full use of technological knowledge.

Post-Independence: In September, 1948 the first and the foremost 'Pilot Project' was started in an area of 64 villages scattered in the vicinity of Maheva near Etawah (U.P.). subsequently in the year 1949, there was again a move for 'Grow more food' campaign with a view to attending self-sufficiency in foodgrains by 1952. The first Five Year Plan conceived the National Extension Service as the agency and community development as the method through which it was envisaged that the successive Five Year Plans would create a better, richer and fuller life for the teeming millions living in thousands of rural communities of India. The National Extension Service was started in 1952 by the Government of India. The Community Development Programme was extended to cover the entire country by a network of 5,265 community development blocks[9]. During the year 1965-66 the Hybrid Seed varieties, which were already supported with proven research results, were chased with high widespread diffusion alongwith the package approach and infrastructure of Intensive Agricultural District Programme.

With the advent of the Fourth Plan in 1969, it was realised by the Planning Commission that ideology of equity in spatial development could not be achieved through adoption of 'ad hoc' and 'piecemeal' planning for urban and rural areas separately. Consequently, realising that the benefits of various development progammes were, in the main, being taken by these better endowed in terms of land resources the programmes especially designed for the development of small and marginal farmers and the landless and agricultural labourers were taken up in the early seventies. A programme of 'food for work' was launched in 1977 and during 1974-77, special sub-plans of development were introduced with a view to removing regional disparities particularly in less endowed or disadvantaged areas, like the hill and tribal areas.

At the close of seventies, it was realised that a small fraction of the rural poor was covered effectively by the various antipoverty programmes. Among the rural poor especially those belonging to the bottom stratum were left untouched. Besides, the territorial overlapping of these programmes and their different funding patterns created considerable difficulties not only in effective monitoring but also thwarted achievements of the programme. In view of these it was decided to combine these programmes into one and designate it as the Integrated Rural Development Programme.

However, based on the above conceptualisation it was, therefore, decided before the start of the Sixth Five Year Plan that the poorest sections belonging to the families of landless labourers, small and marginal farmers, rural artisans, Scheduled Castes/Scheduled Tribes and socially and economically backward classes will have to be assisted through an appropriate package of technologies, services and asset transfer programmes.

Policies and Programmes on Rural Development

The Government of India and the supporters of government policies decided to change the meaning of the concept of 'rural development' after the mid-sixties rural development earlier implied agricultural development and community development enveloping the entire population of rural areas, as a part of modernisation of the under-developed, backward, third world country it mean development which affects the entire population of several areas and enveloping all facets of transformation of rural India as a part of economic growth and modernisation of the whole society. This was the dominant view of 'rural development' till late fifties but has undergone a sea of change since then[10]. However, now rural development is viewed narrowly as a strategy specifically designed to improve the economic and social life of a specific group of rural people, viz, rural poor. The full implication of the changed stance of the state, from viewing rural development process involving both the economic and socio-political development of rural areas as a part of the modernisation of the entire society, to rural development, narrowly defined as strategy focused on specific group, viz' rural poor, as distributive mechanism of overall development, which the rules have adopted, requires closer analysis.

Since it is not possible to analyse in detail the characteristics, limitations of programmes and policies of rural development, we have presented three tables regarding the same in brief. Annexures I and II entitled - (i) "Plan Policies on Rural Development", (ii) "Rural Development Programmes" (from a very thoughtful work by S.R. Maheshwari "Rural Development in India") respectively is reproduced from a journal Voice of Alternative, October, 1986 published from Calcutta.

The adverse economic situation in the country occasioned largely by severe droughts of 1966 and 1967 made the government declare a 'Plan Holiday' and in the place of five year plan, India had three annual plans for 1966-67, 1967-68 and 1968-69. Also the sixties witnessed the Green Revolution consequent to the introduction of new chemical fertilisers and high yielding seed varieties. Rural violence also emerged in many parts of India.

Notes and References

1. Training Strategies for Integrated Rural Development, Asian and Pacific Development Administration Centre, Kuala Lumpur, Malaysia, 1977, pp. 14-15.
2. Susan George (1977), How the other Half Dies, Harpers, New York, Dr. V.K.R.V. Rao, 'Integrated Rural Development', Paper presented at the ADRII of Asian and the Pacific, Third Biennial Conference, Goa, 1977.
3. David A.M. Leo and D.P. Choudhari (1983) Rural Development and the State, Methe London and N.Y., pp. 10-11.
4. Archan Gaur (1985), Integrated Rural Area Development, B.R. Publishing Coporation. Delhi, p. 21.
5. *Ibid*, p. 21.
6. U.P. Goswami, and S.C. Roy (1953), Approaches to Community Development: A Symposium Introductory to Problems and Methods of Village Welfare in Underdeveloped Areas, W. van Hove Ltd., The Hague, p. 310.
7. Vasant Despande (1985), Struggle of the Deprived for Development: 2 (Adivasis of Thane), Distance Ranchandra Co., Pune, p. 14.
8. J.C. Kavoori and B.N. Singh (1967), History of Rural Development in Modern India, p. 14.
9. B.C. Chattopadhyay (1985), Rural Development Planning in India, S. Chand and Co. Ltd., New Delhi, pp. 22-23.
10. A.R. Desai (1987) 'Rural Development and Human Rights in Independent India', Economic and Political Weekly, Aug. 1, pp. 1291- 94.

Annexure I

Plan Policies on Rural Development

Five Year Plan	Political Setting	Policies on Rural Development
1	2	3
First Five Year Plan (1952-56)	Congress party won the election in 1952 under towering personality of Jawaharlal Nehru (Period of political stability).	Community development as method and national Extension Service as the agency.
Second Five Year Plan (1956-61)	Continuance of the Congress party in power at the Centre and in the States (with a few exceptions). Nehru dominance continues.	Cooperative earning; later, local participation

1	2	3
Third Five Year Plan (1961-66)	India receives a serious jolt as a result of the Chinese war (1962). Nehru's stature declines in 1964 he passes away. Corruption in high places confirmed by Santhanam Committee Report (1964), and S.R. Das Report against Pratap Singh Kairou (1966). The Indopak conflict takes place in 1965. Lal Bahadur Shastri who succeeded Nehru as Prime Minister dies and is succeeded by Indira Gandhi, an uncertain political figure at the time.	Panchayatraj, three tier model of democratic decentralisation.
Fouth Five Year Plan (1967-72)	A period of political heterogeneity and fluidity for India. The Congress came into power at the Centre with a much reduced majority, but lost in many states where coalition government of various patterns came into power. In 1969 the Congress was split into the Congress (I) and the Congress (O). The fourteen leading banks were nationalised, initiating an era of populism in politics. The 1971 election was fought and won by the Congress (I) on the plank of 'Garibi Hatao' (removal of poverty).	Special clientele-based and area based programmes.
Fifth Five Year Plan	Populism continues. A politically polarised nation. In 1975 internal emergency imposed, drastically curtailing political and individual rights of the people. In 1977 the Con-	Introduces the concept of basic minimum needs.

1	2	3
	gress party is defeated and the Janata Party came into power. The Janata Government terminates the Fifth Five Year Plan two years early and draft sits own sixth Five year Plan (1978-83).	
Sixth Five Year Plan (1980-85)	The Congress Party returns to power with a massive majority. It abrogates the Janata government's Sixth Five Year Plan and introduces its own Sixth Five Year Plan (1980-85).	Emphasis on strengthening the socio-economic infrastructure in rural areas, alleviateing rural poverty and reducing regional disparities, IRDP
Seventh Five Year Plan (1985-90)	Again Congress Party returns to power under the leadership of Rajiv Gandhi with a massive majority.	Introduce a Major Programme for Rural Poor in merging two Programmes i.e. NREP and RLEGP into one viz. Jawahar Rojgar Yojana

Annexure II
Rural Development Programme

Plan Period	*Programme*	*Year of Introduction*
1	2	3
First Five Year Plan	Community Development Programme	1952
	National Extension Service	1953
Second Five Year Plan	Khadi and Village Industries Programme	1957
	Housing Projects Scheme	1957
	Multi-Purpose Tribal Development Blocks Programme	1959
	Package Programme	1960
Third Five Year Plan	Applied Nutrition Programme	1962
	Rural Industries Projects	1962
	Intensive Agricultural Areas Programme	1964
	High Yielding Variety Programme	1966
Annual Plan 1966	Farmer's Training and Ed. Programme	1966
	Well Construction Programme	1966
Annual Plan 1967	Rural Works Programme (RWP)	1967

1	2	3
Annual Plan 1968	Tribal Development Block	1968
Annual Plan 1969	Rural Manpower Programme	1969
	Composite Programme for Women and Pre. Sch. children	1969
Fourth Five Year Plan	Drough Prone Area Programme	1970
	Cash Scheme for Rural Employment	1971
	Small Farmers' Development Agency (SFDA)	1971
	Tribal Area Development Programme	1972
	Pilot Projects for Tribal Development	1972
	Pilot Intensive Rural Employment Programme	1972
	Minimum Needs Programme	1972
	Command Area Development Programme	1974
Fifth Five Year Plan	Hill Area Development Programme	1975
	ICDC	1975
	Special Livestock Prod. Programme	1975
	Food For Work Programme	1977
	Desert Development Programme	1977
	Whole Village Development Programme	1979
	Training of Rural Youth for Self Employment	1979
	Integrated Rural Development Programme	1979
Sixth Five Year Plan	National Rural Employment Programme	1980
	PM's New Twenty Point Programme	1980
	Development of Women and Children in Rural Areas	1983
Seventh Five Year Plan	Jawahar Rojgar Yojana	1989

2

Decentralization Perspectives and Rural Development

I.C. AWASTHI

I

Decentralization in true sense envisages a revolution of decision-making authority both at the levels of the formulation and the implementation of plan and programmes within the frame-work of a given political structure. It encompasses a field wider than mere administrative evolution which is pragmatic and bureaucratic in nature. In this wider sense, decentralized planning has to adapt to local conditions fully, and influence the local level activities suiting the needs, resource endowments and potential of a particular region. In this type of planning each decision-making unit enjoys autonomy, though there may exist positions of control to co-ordinate various activities within a given structure at the State, District, Block and Village levels. Lastly, it also assumes revolution of financial resources to the local levels.

In the development literature, decentralized planning assumes an important place and rightly so. In the first instance, such planning is a powerful instrument of the effective implementation of planning at a disaggregate level. Secondly, in a country like ours, where almost half of the population is living in abject poverty (particularly in rural areas) and pattern of ownership of assets is concentrated in a few hands, any policy measures have to focus directly upon the target group in particular. This requires involvement of local people with formulation of plans at the micro-levels. Lastly, is such a system of planning, people at large have direct access to resources made available to them as a part of the planning process.

II

It has been experienced that Centralized planning based on usual growth strategy does not offer solution for alleviating widespread poverty and unemployment due to variety of reasons. Hence, it was though necessary to formulate such policy measures as to have direct impact on the problems of poverty and unemployment. The decentralized planning system has, therefore, direct relevance to our socio-economic and political million to subserve the broader social goals. The need of decentralized planning had been felt seriously for implementation of policies and programmes since the inception of planning. The Community Development Programme and the Panchayati Raj institutions were a clear manifestation of faith and belief in the decentralized system of planning. But in practice these institutions have not achieved much operational success due to several deficiencies. Moreover, there has been continuous neglect of local level-planning in reality notwithstanding some half-hearted rhetorics expressed in plan documents. As Trilok Singh points out that "The result of greater accretion of decision-making authority in the Central Ministries has been to thwart initiatives at State level... Rigid adherence to the pattern laid down from above is insisted upon. The IRDP and the other anti-poverty programmes as also the Integrated Tribal Development Projects amply illustrate this fact. Consider for instance, the manner in which DRDA came to be established in all districts".

The existing planning machinery at the district level is week both in terms of technical expertise and financial resources. It has been found that at the district level there are various departments having vertical structure and also several horizontal development agencies exist without having any coordination and linkage among them. There is virtually no such coordinating agency which can take the responsibility to link various existing programmes and schemes so that they can be implemented effectively.

It is, therefore, necessary to build up and strengthen the planning capabilities at the district and block levels. This requires competent planning personnel who could formulate the functions and implement them. These include resources inventory and analysis, formulation of schemes, manpower planning. Budgeting and regular monitoring of the progress of various schemes. This also requires proper integration and linkage with block level planning and district level planning.

To carry out the task of development it is pre-requisite to have a cadre of people dedicated to work at grassroots level and implement various programmes. In this context induction of technical skills through training to various operatives becomes extremely important.

III

The decentralized planning has distinct advantage to poverty removal programme and rural development programmes. It has been felt earlier that planning in general has not produced desired results in raising the standard of living of people. The poverty is on the increase, unemployment assuming serious dimension, disparities are widespread. Though the orientation of planning has been, of late, focussed towards the alleviation of poverty and employment creation programmes for the masses in rural areas in particular, yet a lot is still desired in the way of a change in the attitude of planning system towards the upliftment of poor.

The rural sector is predominant in our economy and urban sector is small. The dualism exists in terms of level development and standard of living of people. The reformer sector constitutes almost three-fourth of population leading subsistence life whereas the latter sector is modern and comparatively leading better life. The rural poverty is no more pronounced constituting small and marginal farmers, landless and agricultural labourers, artisans and those engaged in petty occupations etc. The development planning has accentuated the gap between the two sectors. Regional disparities are increasing in terms of agricultural and industrial development in the rural sector it has rather created social imbalances and given birth to a powerful elite class having enormous influence in the rural power structure. The benefits of development accrue to this class because it owns most of the assets, skills, education and other resources. The poor are thus left out from the mainstream of development. Therefore, the planning strategy has to become structural rather than mere allocational and decentralized planning assumes an important place in this direction and needs to be strengthened so that it becomes more effective vehicle of social transformation. No planning efforts can be sustained for long unless it alleviates poverty. The alleviation of poverty requires concerted efforts and is closely interlined to the asset distribution and generation programmes rather than mere distribution of income.

We have planning system having decentralization philosophy within the centralized planning which is not effective. The basic difficulty is that our political leadership and planners have, time and again, been stressing the need of having decentralized planning for effective implementation of planning for various reason — political and economic compulsions — without giving up the bias towards centralized philosophy of planning. Therefore, seeking the benefits of decentralization without significant decentralization on the one hand and on the other hand strong centralized philosophy have been detrimental to the spirit of decentralization.

The decentralized planning has to become an integral part of and consistent with the overall planning. In this sense the decentralized planning is compatible within the framework of centralized planning. There are certain areas of activities where centralization becomes inevitable especially in the context of industrialization process another vital areas of scientific and technological development. On the other hand to make planning more effective and realistic it is necessary to have decentralization of planning. In reality there is no contradiction between centralization and decentralization as such. Rather both are complimentary.

IV

The success of decentralized planning largely depends on how these various programmes are implemented. This required peoples involvement in each stage. The local-level planning has an advantage that it provide an adequate degree of participation of people in the formulation and implementation process. The participation of local-level people assures better implementation at all levels because they have an intimate knowledge of local conditions.

Theoretically the above argument is true but in practice it has generally been experienced that at the local level only a few influential persons rule the entire population. This class of influential persons comprising elite class, monied class, property owners and also from upper castes have the advantage of taking part in the various development activities. The rest of the population (forming a major part of the total population) have virtually no access at all in the participation in various development schemes. This is mainly because that a large part of the population is illiterate, poor, ignorant about their rights and non-organized. In such cases it is likelihood that the benefits of development efforts would largely accrue to the former class. For instance digging an irrigation canal would benefit those having large size of land holding who can make use of irrigation facilities rather than marginal/poor farmers who have a little piece of land or no land.

The basic question here arises that whose participation we are envisaging in the planning process at the grass-root level? Is it for the group of a few influential persons who have every access in the process of participation in the formulation of development schemes and who intern appropriate the large benefits thereof or the poor people who are helpless and for whom the planning is supposed to be an instrument for their upliftment?

The question if local initiatives or participation at the local level in practice leaves much to be desire for percolation of planning efforts. The Planning Commission's working group 1877 (under the chairmanship of M.L. Dantwala) has also raised serious doubts about the involvement of the poor people at the grass-root level planning in our socio-economic framework.

The pre-requisite of successful decentralized planning is, therefore, to create a proper environment to bring a kind of attitudinal change among the poor people towards the various development activities meant for them; to make them conscious about their rights through various educational programmes and through audio-visual aids at the local levels. The bureaucracy— the various functionaries from the district level to village level—has to be made responsible to their function. Their role ought not be merely to formulate and implement programmes but also to ensure that the benefits of these development efforts are made available to the poor people.

References

1. Trilok Singh, 'Decentralization and Execution in the Seventh Plan' in Seventh Plan Perspective, Malcolm S. Adiseshiah (ed.) Lancer International 1985, pp. 304-7 at p. 304.
2. C.T. Kuries 'Decentralization Perspective in the Seventh Plan' in Seventh Plan Perspectives, Malcolm S. Adiseshiah (ed) Lancer International 1985, pp. 283-303 at p. 286.
3. Moonis Raza 'Regional Disparities and Decentralization' in Seventh Plan' in Seventh Plan Perspectives, Malcolm S. Adiserhiah (ed) Lancer International 1985, pp. 313-18.
4. Amritananda Das 'Decentralization of Development Planning and Implementation' in The Indian Journal of Public Administrator Special

Number, July Sept., 1978, Vol. XXIV, No. 3, pp. 557-70 at p. 557.

5. M.A. Muttalib 'Decentralization: A New Philosophy of Corporate Life' in The Indian Journal of Public Administration, Special Number, July - Sept., 1978, Vol. XXIV, No. 3, pp. 702-9 at pp. 703-9.
6. Moonis Raza, *op, cit.*, p. 320.

3

Rural Development and Employment Policies in India

MUKTA MITTAL AND ASHOK KUMAR

Rural development, of late, has become a global concern, though issues involved in it continue to suffer from ambiguity and lack of direction. It is the current range among planning experts and policy-makers as a solution to the problems of poverty in developing countries. In India, progressive reduction of unemployment has been one of the principal objectives of economic planning. It was, therefore, felt necessary in the different plans to have supplemental programmes for specific target groups/areas for employment creation; income generation and poverty alleviation. These have taken the form of direct employment programmes for providing seasonal employment to agricultural labourers on rural capital works and beneficiary/target-group-oriented programmes of asset provision, input deliveries and marketing and credit infrastructure creation.

It is felt that the agricultural sector alone cannot be expected to eliminate the backlog of unemployment and absorb the additions to the labour force. The rate of industrial growth must be accelerated. But as experience has shown, even a high rate of industrial growth would not be able to create additional employment to absorb more than a fraction of the unemployed and under employed labour forces in the organized industrial sector. Therefore, programmes of development and in particular, of massive rural capital formation the form of construction become necessary. This strategy would also help to raise the rate of growth of agriculture. Further, it would increase the incomes and purchasing power of the weaker segments of the population and thereby provide the demand support to the growth process.

At the beginning of the Seventh Plan, it was estimated that 222 million persons or 38 per cent population in rural India lived below the poverty line. These rural poor consist largely of the landless, marginal farmers and other marginal workers. In order to reduce unemployment and the incidence of rural poverty, three broad policy options have been pursued. First, assistance for creation of better productive asset base have been introduced. Second, augmentation of wage incomes has been sought through expansion of employment in agricultural and non-agricultural activities in the rural areas, and thirdly, special employment generation programmes have been initiated to provide supplementary employment. Besides, special programmes or provide opportunities for betterment of life have been developed for the specially disadvantaged groups like, Scheduled Castes and Scheduled Tribes and Women.

However, keeping in view the relevance and importance of employment policy for rural development an attempt has been made in this paper to give an account of the employment trends and changing occupational pattern in rural India. The focus is made primarily on the rural employment programmes developed so far for the employment generation. During Sixth and Seventh Five Year Plans how far these programmes have generated employment in the rural areas and different issues arising of this will be discussed. And finally, recommendations have been made for some policy alternatives for effectively increasing rural employment and for alleviating their present day low status.

Recent Trends

(i) Estimates of unemployment: Information is available on labour force participation rates and unemployment rates based on the 32nd round (pertaining to 1977-78) in the National Sample Survey Organization Study on employment-unemployment (also used in Sixth Plan document) and from the 38th round (pertaining to 1983 for the first two sub-rounds thereof covering the period January - June 1983).

The estimate of usual status unemployment as at the beginning of the Seventh Plan, based on the relevant rates from the 32nd round survey are given in Table 1 for different age -groups and with sex/location break up.

Table 1

Estimates of Unemployment (usual status) in March, 1985 on the basis of 32nd Round

Category		*Age group* (5+)	(15+)	*(In Million)* (15,59)
Rural	Males	3.74	3.56	3.52
	Females	4.06	3.77	3.71
Urban	Males	3.65	3.56	3.52
	Females	2.44	2.36	2.35
	Total	13.89	13.25	13.10

It would be useful to have estimates of backlog of unemployment based on more recent survey information (on 38th round) not withstanding the fact that this is partial and provisional. These estimates are given in Table 2 for the different age-group and with sex/location breakup.

It is seen that the estimate of unemployment (usual status) in March, 1985 as per the latest information is 9.20 million for the age-group 5 plus. A proper comparison of this estimate is at the beginning of 1985 based on the most recent survey data with the estimate at the beginning of March, 1980 in the Sixth Plan document will have to await fuller information from the other two sub-rounded of 38th round. Going on the basis of this estimate of unemployment, the overall magnitude to be generated during the Seventh Plan period works out to 48.58 million for the age-group 5 plus.

Table 2

Estimates of Unemployment (usual status) in March, 1985 on the basis of 38th Round

Category		*Age group* (5+)	(15+)	*(In Million)* (15,59)
Rural	Males	3.76	3.54	3.49
	Females	1.21	1.13	1.10
Urban	Males	3.25	3.14	3.12
	Females	0.98	9.96	0.96
	Total	**9.20**	**8.77**	**8.67**

(ii) *Changes in Occupation Structure:* Over a decade, there has been a decline in the self-employment in relation to casual labour, with the proportion of the regular salaries wage worker remaining more or less constant. An important trend to be noted in this context is a change in structure of the work-force. There has been a shift from rural to urban areas and more strikingly, within the rural areas there is a shift from agriculture to non-agricultural activities, as can be seen from the following figures of percentage of workers in agricultural activities in 1972-73, 1977-78 and 1983.

The spread of commercialization and greater agricultural prosperity have led to the expansion of non-agricultural activities leading to diversification of the rural economy. At the same time both the 'push' and 'pull' factors were strong enough to divert the additional labour force into non-agricultural activities. This is because the agricultural activity has shown negative marginal productivity, making it unprofitable. At the same time opportunity cost of the agricultural worker, has been turned into zero. While definite indicators are not yet available, it is likely that both trends are at work in the different regions of the economy. This shift in any case, is notable for the purposes of future strategies and programmes for rural development.

Table 3

Percentage Changes in Occupational Structure

		Agriculture		*Non-Agriculture*	
		Male	*Female*	*Male*	*Female*
Usual States	1972-73	83.23	89.67	16.77	10.33
	1977-78	80.60	88.10	19.40	11.90
	1983	76.80	86.73	23.20	13.27
Current Daily States	1972-73	—	—	—	—
	1977-78	78.15	83.23	21.85	16.77
	1983	73.29	79.07	26.71	29.93

Source: Sarvekshana, Vol. IX, No. 4, April, 1986.

Review of Measures Initiated for Employment Generation in Rural Areas.

The main programmes through which employment is to be

generated in the rural areas are:

— National Rural Employment Programme (NREP)
— Integrated Rural Development Programme (IRDP)
— Rural Landless Employment Guarantee Programme (RLEGP)
— Training Rural Youth for Self Employment (TRYSEM)
— Self Employment to Educated Unemployed Youth, and
— Special Employment Programmes of States.

(i) *National Rural Employment Programme (NREP):* This programme aims at generating employment opportunities in the rural areas, simultaneously creating durable community assets for strengthening the rural infrastructure, it also seeks to improve the nutritional status and living standards of the rural poor. The programme operates in close conjunction with other development works. For the Sixth Five Year Plan, there was a provision of Rs. 980 crores in the central sector and Rs. 640 crores in the states sector making a total of Rs. 1,620 crores for this programme. The progress of employment generating as a result of the execution of various works under the programme has been as follows:

Table 4

Generation of Employment

Year	Target	(In million mandays) Achievements
1980-81	—	413.58
1981-82	335.73	354.57
1982-83	353.22	350.10
1983-84	322.23	302.02
1984-85	309.13	349.90

(ii) *Rural Landless Employment Guarantee Programme (RLEGP):* It was felt (during the Sixth Plan) that the hardcore rural poverty, particularly that pertaining to the unemployment of the landless labourers during the lean agricultural season, had to be tackled in a more direct manner, Accordingly a new scheme called the RLEGP was introduced in 1983. The basic objectives of the programme are: (a) to improve and expand employment opportunities for rural landless with a view to providing guarantee of employment to at least one member of every landless labour household upto 100 days in a year; and (b) creation of durable assets for strengthening the rural infrastructure which will lead to rapid growth of the rural economy. Assistance under the programme was provided to the State/UT Governments on 100 per cent grant basis. Funds amounting to Rs. 600 crores were allocated to them in the last two years of the Sixth Plan. It originally expected that 360 million mandays of employment would be generated under the programme during the last two years of the Sixth Plan Period, i.e. during 1983-85. However, as against this 260.15 million mandays of employment were generated during these years.

(iii) *Integrated Rural Development Programme (IRDP):* It is the single largest scheme for providing direct assistant to the rural poor and is meant for the poorest among the poor. Its objective is to provide productive assets and employment to the poor for enabling them to attain higher incomes and a better standard of living. The IRDP was expected to over 15 million families to be identified in all the blocks of the country during the Sixth Plan period on an average, 3000 families in a block were to be provided assistance through this programme. A sum of Rs. 1,500 crores was provided in the plan outlay for this programme. The banks were called upon to provide another Rs. 3.000 by way of loans to selected beneficiaries. Further, back-up facilities in infrastructure community projects and assistance to voluntary agencies were also provided.

(iv) *Training Rural Youth for Self-employment (TRYSEM)* : This scheme was initiated in 1979 with the principal objective of removing unemployment among the rural youth. The target was to train about 2 lakh rural youth every year at the rate of 40 youth per block of the country. The TRYSEM is an integrated part of the IRDP and aims at equipping the rural youth with skilled to enable them to become self-employed. A rural youth from a family having an income of less than Rs. 3,500 per year was eligible for selection. Preference in selection was given to those who had aptitude for innovation and entrepreneurial activities. Priority was also given to members of SC/ST and women. The accepted model of available information, 9.4 lakh rural youth received training under TRYSEM during the Sixth Plan. Around 50 per cent of them have taken up self-employment.

(v) *Self-employment to Educated Unemployed Youth* : The Scheme was introduced in 1983 for providing self-employment to educated unemployed youth. The scheme provides for the grants of loan up to a maximum of Rs. 25,000 to educated youth residing in areas other than cities with a population of 10 lakhs or more and having no other source of finance for setting down in self-employment. The implementation of the scheme was entrusted to the District Industries Centre (DIC) under the guidance of the Development Commissioner for Small Scale Industries. As allocation of Rs. 25 crores was made for the programme during 1984-85 in the central budget to cover Government assistance in the shape of an outright capital subsidy to the extent of 25 per cent of the loans taken by the entrepreneurs from the banks.

(vi) Some State Governments are implementing Special Employment Schemes to provide additional employment opportunities. The Employment Guarantee Scheme (EGS) of Maharashtra operating since 1972, is intended to provide employment on productive works to the workers desirous of rendering unskilled manual work and thereby reduce the rendering unskilled manual work and thereby reduce the incidence of unemployment, underemployment and poverty in rural areas. The State Government gave a statutory backing to the guarantee of employment through the Employment Guarantee Act, 1977. The guarantee of work is restricted to unskilled manual work. In 1983-84, 164.5 million mandays of employment were reported to have been generated . There are also schemes by other State Governments for the benefit of the unemployed whereby training, financial assistance and other incentives are provided.

Related Issues

The above official statistics shows that a substantial number of mandays have been generated through different employment programmes. However, based on some recent studies following issues emerged:

- Technological changes have led to increases in field and cropping intensities but at the same time, these have also been labour displacing. Hence, the additions to the labour force will have to find employment in non-agricultural activates. The possibility of the non-agricultural sector to absorb the increasing supply of labour will depend on the level of rural demand for non-agricultural goods and services produced locally.
- Non-agricultural employment has experienced a significant growth during the recent past decades leading to a notable diversification of rural employment. Available evidence suggests that the rural manufacturing enterprises are growing larger and turning from the household to the non-household sector, hence, creating opportunities for wage labour to a certain extent. The expansion of markets both for inputs and outputs is also seen to lead to a shift in location of certain

rural manufacturing activities from villages to the nearby towns.

— In those areas which are characterized by a more backward agriculture, there is considerable scope for increasing on farm employment. In those states where changes in cropping patterns have been in favour of the relatively more labour intensive crops (e.g. traditional paddy, groundnut and cotton) and there has been an increase in gross cropped area and area under irrigation, the total employment effect is positive.

— Improved agro-processing techniques including marketing and distribution have high direct and indirect labour demand and the scheme of planning for agro-climatic regions attempts to provide for these features.

— More priority has been given in the Plan to Special Employment and Area Oriented Programmes. These programmes are being monitored and evaluated on a continuous basis and effort at streaming them and integrating them with small farmer and landless labour population will continue.

— Land Reforms Programmes need to be given very high priority. Attentions is being paid to this aspect at the highest political levels.

— In the implementation of rural development progammes like the IRDP, NREP and RLEGP the emerging trends in the structures of activities and labour force as indicated earlier need to be kept in view. More particularly, the trends in the diversification of the rural economy into the non-agricultural sectors need to be utilized with advantage, and the need for wage employment for longer period for the poor and increasing number of casual wage labours needs to be recognised.

Employment Potential in Rural Areas

Substantial employment would be generated in rural areas through:

(i) development of irrigated farming and optimum utilization of the irrigation potential;

(ii) propagation of thé available technologies in dry land/rain-fed farming;

(iii) special programmes for increasing the production of rice, coarse grains, pulses and oil seeds;

(iv) special programmes for land stock improvement for the utilization of cultivable wastelands and areas suffering from various problems like alkalinity, salinity and water-logging;

(v) intensification of horticulture development in hill or tribal areas and also in wastelands and dry regions:

(vi) acceleration of the programmes relating to animal husbandry and dairy farming;

(vii) expansion of activities in the fisheries sector for tapping the vast production potential; and

(viii) intensification of developmental activity in afforestation.

However, generation of gainful employment opportunities is the most arduous and highly challenging task. For successful training, all resources have to be pooled gather and all connected agencies have to come together and all connected agencies have to come together.

Notes and References

1. Subramaniam, C. (1983): 'A Strategy for Rural Development' in the (ed.) book' 'Studies on Rural Development', by Ajit K. Danda'm IIPA, New Delhi, p. 25.
2. The Seventh Five Year Plan 1985-90, Volume II, Government of India, Planning Commission, New Delhi, October 1985.
3. *Ibid;* Mid-Term Appraisal.
4. This concept is meant to measure the usual activity status employed or unemployed or outside the labour force of those covered by the survey; the activity status is determined with reference to a longer period than a day or a week, in the preceding 365 days.
5. Mid-Term Appraisal of 7th five year Plan 1985-90, Government of India, Planning Commission.

4

Poverty, Unemployment and Manpower Planning: Concepts and Definitions

RAJENDRA P. MAMGAIN

Introduction

In most of the developing countries population is growing fastly, due to which these nations are facing number of problems. These countries are generally characterized as with low per capita income, increasing unequal distribution of national product, poor financial resources for tapping the available physical resources, low capital formation. Low standard of living resulting in low level of health, high rate of illiteracy etc. In the words of Reguar Nurkes vicious circles are in operation in these countries.

In such types of situations where population grows fastly and available resources are not sufficient to meet the requirements of the population are juxtaposed to above mentioned problems. In these economies capital formation is insufficient to absorb the excess labour force. Thus, labour force basically depends on agriculture sector which finally shows its inability to absorb more labour. This results in zero marginal productivity. For industries again there is a lack of resources for which they have to depend on foreign aids flow from developed countries.

Thus, with these complex situations in developing countries where employment opportunities are not bright leads population into the state of more poverty and unemployment. These two concepts are very important in the literature of development economics. Oftenly economists are not of the same opinion regarding the concept of poverty and unemployment, which has been discussed in detail in the following sections. But one thing is very clear that these two are major challenge for a welfare society. Prolonged existence of poverty and unemployment may become the severe challenge to any ruling political party's survival and country's independence may be in danger. The term manpower planning has also been narrated in detail. It can been observed from the ongoing discussion that manpower planning is an integral part of economic planning. As economic planning is made to remove poverty and unemployment, manpower planning is necessary to achieve it.

Concept of Poverty

Poverty is such a concept which is closely related to inequality and makes a base for comparing two extremes of inequality. Given the average income level, a higher level of inequality (reflected by the usual measures) will tend to be associated with a higher level of poverty. Furthermore, the so called poverty line, may some times be drawn in the light of socially accepted 'minimal' standard of living, and the later can be influenced by the average income level, so that poverty measures, thus defined may catch an aspect of 'relative' inequality as well.

There are however, two major problems involved in defining the concept of poverty. The first relates to the problem of identifying the 'poor' and second is the 'problem of measurement'.

Economists consider poverty purely and economic concept. They define the concept of poverty broadly in terms of (i) economic inequality (of income/wealth and /or command over resources), (ii) nutritional deficiency or malnutrition, (iii) deficiency of basic minimum needs, and (iv) insufficiency of income to meet socially (or otherwise) accepted minimum needs. An economic concept of poverty generally involves a cut-off point/norm (commonly known as poverty line) which may be relative (as in case of poverty as economic inequality) or an absolute one.

There are number of concepts presented time-to-time on concepts and measurement of poverty. Notable among them are as follows. Rowntree (1899) was the first in Britain to consider in detail the problem involved in defining poverty, and clearly saw his approach as being based on absolute line. According to him a family was considered to be living in poverty if its total earnings were insufficient to obtain the minimum necessaries for the maintenance of merely physical requirement.

Townsend (1970) was of the opinion that there is no distinction between relative and absolute poverty and suggests that 'poverty must be regraded as a general form of relative deprivation which is the effect of the maldistribution of resources' and that section of the population whose resources are so depressed from the means as to be deprived of enjoying the benefits and participating in the activities which are customary in that society can be said to be in poverty. This is not the same thing as saying that the poor are 10 per cent or 20 per cent in every society with the least resources.

Martin Rein (1970) argued that three broad concepts of poverty can be identified viz. Subsistence, inequality and externality. Subsistence is concerned with the minimum provision needed to maintain health and working capacity... inequality is concerned with the relative position of the income groups to each other... The concept of poverty must be seen in the context of society as a whole.... Externality is concerned with the social consequence of poverty for the rest of the society rather than in terms of the needs of the poor.

Dorothy Wedderburn (1974) however followed the same approach of Martin Rein and defined the poverty as when the individuals, families and groups in the society lack the basic resources to obtain the types of diets, participate in the activities and have the living conditions and amenities which are customary, or are atleast, widely encouraged or approved in the societies to which they belong. They are having very scarce resources to maintain the minimum standard of living, customs resources to maintain the minimum standard of living, customs and activities. Wedderburn is of the opinion that the terms i.e. property and inequality are closely interrelated and needs to be considered in turn. Although poverty is more than inequality, the poor undoubtedly receive and unequal share of resources and any explanation of this fact must be related to the larger explanation or social inequality in general.

Some economists based their approach on nutritional deficiency while defining poverty. In 1971 Dendekar and Rath while basing their approach on nutritional deficiency stated that an annual per capita expenditure of at least Rs. 170 at 1960-61 prices was necessary to provide a minimum diet of just 2553 calories. If per capita expenditure is less than the above minimum line, the person is said to be poor.

The approach of Reserve Bank of India (R.B.I.) is somewhat slightly different in defining poor. According to R.B.I. report on All India Debt and Investment survey of 1971-72, the poor peasants, landless labourers and other landless households have been identified as the rural poor. But here one basic question is that why and how are they called or identified as poor? An attempt has been made in R.B.I.'s 1971-72 report to identify the rural poor on the basis of the asset-holding criterion; all household possessing assets below Rs. 2,500 are identified as poor. The average physical assets per household of these rural poor amounted to Rs. 987, and they account for more than one third of rural population. If a household operation from 2.49 acres of holding is defined as poor, than NSSO 26th Round of 1971-72 shows that a little more than 60 per cent of the total number of rural households fall in this category.

But the asset and land holding criteria of poverty measurement may not be given the extent to which a household is unable to fulfill the basic living requirements, such as food, clothing and shelter. Most of the studies have followed the per capita consumption expenditure approach in defining poverty.

Though most of the studies have taken per capita consumption expenditure as a measuring rod of poverty, but this approach is also not free from its shortcomings. In most of developing countries like India growth of G.N.P. is considered an important indicator of economic development and well being. For the first time Gunnar Myrdel challenged this notion and observed that if inequality is increasing with the growth of G.N.P. total socio economic well being may be at lower. It is also well established point that per capita income always determines the level of per capita expenditure. Thus, in the above mentioned case where G.N.P. increases with its unequal distribution relative poverty also increase. Poor's per capita expenditure on consumption necessities is higher than the rich, so it may not be wise to say that this much of minimum amount of per capita consumption expenditure is necessary. Rich people' per capita expenditure is higher in the case of luxuries etc.

This is why Dendekar and Rath (1971) has correctly stated that "the problem of poverty in India is a problem of low national income and its unequal distribution, of slow pace of development and inequitable distribution of the small gains of development".

Thus, it can be seen from the above definition part that scholars are not of the single opinion regarding the definition of poverty. This is why the poverty estimates are divergent in our country. Broadly speaking, poverty is classified into two categories, viz., absolute and relative. Absolute poverty has been defined in terms of nutritional deficiency, lack of basic necessities of life or as a problem of want and deprivation. Relative poverty is defined in terms of level of income. Level of standard of living etc. A person is called relatively poor when his present level of income etc. is below than another person.

Bhatty (1974) stated that both absolute and relative poverty are closely aligned to inequality in income distribution. Relative poverty is mainly due to an unequal distribution of income irrespective of what the income level. Or the corresponding state of deprivation of the people at the bottom end of the income scale might be. Absolute poverty, on the other hand, expresses a collective view as deprivation in its somewhat physical manifestation.

Absolute Poverty

Poverty in an absolute sense has been defined in various studies in three different ways. In terms of nutritional deficiency and malnutrition a person is considered poor if he does not get the minimum required calories from his food basket or he is unable to get the minimum desired quantity of other nutrients. However this approach suffers from many drawbacks. Nutritional intake varies from region to region, person to person, season to season. So it may be unwise to say a person poor who infact is not taking desired nutrients due to bad income/habits and on the other hand is having more income. Thus, here may be underestimation of poverty.

Poverty as Want and Deprivation

In absolute sense poverty has also been defined as 'lack of basic necessities of life' or as a problem of deprivation from the basic needs. For a simple living a person needs food, clothing, shelter etc. Education further develops the inherent qualities of a person and may further contribute to inherent qualities of a person and may further contribute to improve present standard of living. Health status mainly depends on the extent of the fulfilment of basic needs. Thus, the whole chain is like that if a person is deprived from the fulfilment of three basic necessities he will also be deprived from education, health and consequently income. Many reasons may be attributed for being a person deprived from basic necessities viz., very low per capita income, skewed distribution of national income, lack of employment opportunities, large family size mainly depending on uneconomic activities etc. high proportion of child and old population.

Practically it is difficult to measure poverty on the basis of deprivation. To know that how long a person is/was deprived from the minimum basis necessities it becomes necessary to collect the information on different aspects from which a person is deprived. This information is to be collected from all deprived persons through a comprehensive survey and then to develop a 'deprivation index system' with standardized weighing procedure. No doubt this is an arduous work but it can be done regional as well as sample basis. While the norms for all stocks and flows can not be in quantitative terms. We will have to depend on monetary weights equivalent to their share in the total consumption basket of consumer. The approach then essentially is akin to the poverty line approach.

Absolute Poverty Line Approach

In the literature of poverty the most commonly term is 'poverty line'. This term was first used by Arthur Young. But the more scientifically this term is used by Charles Booth (1989), in England. According to the poverty line approach persons living below the prescribed norms will be called poor. The main question here is how to draw such a line? What should be the considerations in fixing the minimum amount of income resources needed? These are very ticklish issues on which opinions widely differ.

Charles Booth (1989) has suggested that the poverty line be drawn at an income level where "means may be sufficient but are barely sufficient for independent life." Thus Booth's poor are those who "are struggling to obtain the necessaries of life and make both ends meet". Booth draws another poverty line for every poor' whose means are insufficient for them according to the usual standard of life in the country. They are living in the state of chronic want. Thus according to the poverty line approach if a person's means are insufficient to meet the minimal level of living, which are just sufficient to live, will be said living in poverty line. The poverty line may vary, country to country.

Thus, it is clear from the above conceptual part of the poverty that economists are not unanimous about the notion of poverty. Hence poverty estimates are varied while estimating poverty due to different approaches. These estimates are biased and the literature on poverty needs further indepth scientific study so to make correct estimates of poverty.

What is Unemployment

To those who have not given much thought to the subject, it would appear easy to define unemployment, but the fact is that this is far from being the case. For example, many people who would not call themselves "unemployed" are certainly 'underemployed', that is, they would be glad to undertake more work if they could get it. At what point does under-employment lapse into unemployment? Again is a man to be considered unemployed who is practically unemployable. If so, is a man who has worked steadily during all his life, but grown too old for further work, to be counted among the unemployed? If not, way could among them a young man who, through some physical defect, is no more employable then the veteran of labour? Again is a man to be counted unemployed who is ill, but whose employment is waiting for him when he recovers? Or is a trade unionist to be counted unemployed who can not find work at the trade union rate of wages, but who could do so if he could accept a farthing an hour less, or who could not find work in Punjab but could in Haryana if he could go there? These illustration which might readily be multiplied, will serve to show how difficult it is to define unemployment precisely; and how easy it would be to compile statistics of it which might be very misleading.

Concept of Unemployment

The concepts of unemployment has been defined in different fashion by economists and others from time to time. According to one it is "a state of affairs in which for various reasons, men have to remain without jobs over many months or even for a longer period". Unemployment denotes the existence of a reserve of labour time available for utilization . This "reserve may be visible and/or invisible. Visible unemployment is indicative of the manhours of work which in existing conditions, the labour force is willing but unable to perform. In short it is synonymous with enforced idleness".

In the pre-Keynesian literature, this problem of unemployment has received lot of attention from economists and since 1935 when Lord Keynes published his 'General Theory', unemployment is thought of as the outcome of depressions. Apart from fractional and seasonal types, it was broadly conceived to be associated with the business cycles. Keynes, however distinguished a new category what he called "involuntary unemployment" which might and as a rule, did exist even under boom conditions. According to Keynes insufficiency of 'effective demand' was the root cause of unemployment.

The ILO (1961) has defined the term "employed" and "unemployed" as follows:

"The employed' should include all persons who work on their own account or are in the employment of others. The employed should thus include employers, persons who are self-employed (i.e., who work on their own account), salaries employees, wage earners and unpaid family workers who are engaged in tasks directly related to operation of a family enterprise for a minimum of at least one-third of the normal working time during the specified period of week, not including hours spent in unpaid domestic work. 'The employed' should include persons. In labour camps if they are free to seek alternative employment, but should not include persons in such camps who are not free to make the choice; or persons confined to prisons or similar institutions. Persons who are directly employed by any public authority or emergency public relief. Work should also be included in the statistics of the employed but where such persons are employed under conditions inferior to those of regular public-employees engaged in the same type of work, their number should be indicated separately.

"The 'unemployed' should include all persons seeking work on a given day, who are not employed but are able to take a job if offered one".

"Labour force should include all 'employed' as well as 'unemployed persons', as defined above, together with the armed forces. The civilian Labour Force should include all employed and unemployed persons exclusive of the armed forces".

It the above definitions no mention has been made about the hours of work or income required to classify an 'on own account' worker, employer or employee as engaged in full time work. Seasonal employments, too, have not been considered. The concept of employment which is a unique characteristic of majority of workers in rural areas in the country has not been dealt with at all. Thus, the concepts propounded may be all right for certain countries with organized economies but they cannot be used in assessing unemployment and under-employment in the country like India.

Underemployment

The Ninth International Conference of Labour Statisticians in a resolution made the following observations about the 'Underemployment :'

"Underemployment exists when persons in employment who are not working full time would be able and willing to do more work than they are actually performing, or when the income or productivity of persons in employment would be raised if they worked under improved conditions of production or transferred to another occupation, account being taken of their special skill".

The resolutive mentions in particular two categories of underemployment, viz.

(a) Visible underemployment , which involves shorter than normal periods of work and which is characteristics of persons involuntarily working part-time.

(b) Invisible underemployment which is characteristics of persons whose working time is not abnormally reduced but whose earnings are abnormally low or where jobs do not permit full use of their capacities or skills (sometimes called disguised unemployment) or who are employed in establishment, of economic units where productivity is abnormally low (sometimes called potential unemployment).

Type of Unemployment

It becomes imperative to understand the nature and type of unemployment before going to suggest any ramifications. Economists do not use one and the some terms cannot a given situation, it is essential to define certain important terms used by the. Broadly unemployment can be put as in the following way:

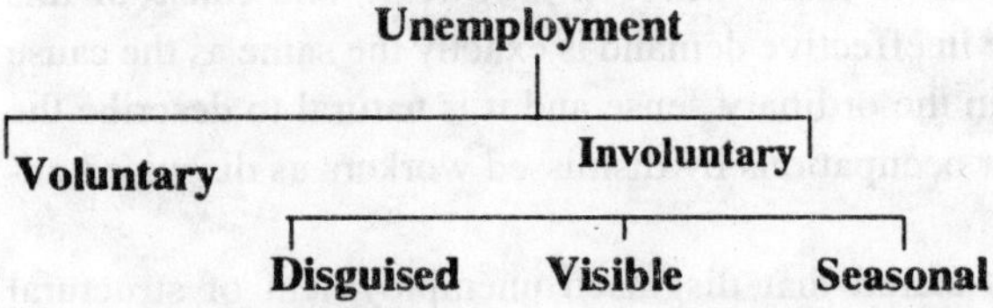

Voluntary Unemployment

This may be defined as the unemployment which results from the withdrawal of same persons from employment for diverse reasons such as (i) absence of need to earn when one has already made fortune, or when one inherits a large amount of wealth or property so as to have means of livelihood for a considerable time; (ii) social custom of certain groups to discourage or forbid engagement of certain members in

productive work, e.g., the "purdah system" (keeping behind the curtain closed from the outside world) which is still in vogue among certain upper middle, class women in India, leads to their voluntary unemployment; and (iii) lethargy or obstinacy, etc. In fact, voluntary unemployment under unemployment is a misnomer as there may be 'idle rich' and also 'idle poor' who refuse to work of their own second. However, for policy purposes, voluntary unemployment has hardly any significance.

Involuntary Unemployment

For the policy-making purposes, voluntary unemployment is important. This may be defined as the unemployment due to non availability or insufficiency of work during periods of, say, a few weeks, a few months, or even a few years when the workers in question want to work. Following the general practice among different modern economists, it would be appropriate to use the term 'unemployment' only in the sense of involuntary unemployment. It may take various forms disguised, visible and seasonal.

Disguised Unemployment

The term disguised unemployment was first used by Mrs. John Robinson (1936) for referring to the workers having low rathér than zero marginal product of labour due to the cyclical transfer of persons from the more productive to less productive jobs during industrial recession. She observes that "a decline in demand for the product of the general run of industries leads to a diversion of labour from occupations in which productivity is higher to those where it is lower". The cause of this diversion, a decline in effective demand is exactly the same as the cause of unemployment in the ordinary sense and it is natural to describe the adoption of inferior occupations by dismissed workers as disguised unemployment.

Nurkse (1955) stated that disguised unemployment of structural variety will prevail where a number of people are working on farms of small peasant plots, contributing virtually nothing to output, but living of a share of their family's net income. In technical terms, the marginal productivity of labour over a wide range is zero.

Visible Unemployment

Visible unemployment is rather a simple concept. It means, for all practical purposes, the total absence of jobs for workers for some period.

The term may refer either to those who have been thrown out of employment due to a fall in the demand for the products of an industry or any other occupation or it may refer to the new entrants to the labour market who have to remain out of employment for some time due to lack of jobs.

Seasonal Unemployment

This is perhaps the oldest concept in the employment/unemployment literature. Seasonal unemployment may be defined as the lack of productive work during some periods of the year or as just seasonal idleness. This kind of unemployment arised mainly from the dependence of certain occupations or industries or climatic conditions. Unemployment in the ice-manufacturing industry of a tropical county in the winter season may be cited as an example.

Other Types of Unemployment

Technological Unemployment : This is somewhat complex. Nevertheless, it could be roughly defined as a situation 'when the given output catering for a constant level of demand is produced by a lesser number of workers owing to the adoption of improved technologies; and consequently, the new surplus workers become unemployed. This form of unemployment, normally occurs in advanced industrial economies, where there is a considerable emphasis on technological research.

Cyclical Unemployment of Keynesian Type : The concept of full employment propounded by classical economists was first time questioned by Keynes in his General Theory (1936). According to Kenynes there always occurs unemployment in any form in a economy. Due to the inadequate effective demand largely emerging from excess savings in the short-run, results in an under-employment equilibrium where a part of the labour force has to remain involuntary unemployed. As soon effective demand increases, under given conditions, with every rise in the real income than the mounting disparity between exante savings and ex-ante investments disappears. Then according to Keynes, an upward movement towards full employment ensues.

Structural Unemployment : Assuming a prior condition of shortage of capital, this type of unemployment is a peculiar characteristic of over-populated under-developed countries. Structural unemployment can be defined as one which occurs as a result of an inappropriate balance of race course. It can arise in two conditions. First, when investments fails to follow in appropriate directions and second, when labour supply is maladjusted in relation to skill and location.

Shadow Unemployment : Data available on unemployment do not take account of those persons who leave the present pool of labour force for lack of economic opportunity. Old people and married women may no longer actually look for work due to tight job market, but if the job market becomes easy they may re-enter the labour force.

Meaning of Manpower

'Manpower is that part of total human resources which bears a more significant correlation with economic growth than the homogeneous labour input, largely due to the interaction of factors like education, training and acquisition of skill, technical innovation and increasing poverty; Trained manpower is more dynamic than the labour input and does not merely represent skilled labour.

Definition of Manpower Planning

Manpower planning has been defined as "the process of developing and determining objectives, policies and programmes that will develop, utilize and distribute manpower so as to achieve economic and other goals. It includes developing the necessary organizations and institution required to execute manpower programmes. The excellent Department of Employment booklet has defined manpower planning as "a strategy for the acquisition, utilization, improvement and retention of an enter-prise's human resources". 'Strategy' implies a change in the management of manpower from the tactical approach that is probably most common. It raises the prospects of determining objectives, with the implication of an intention to meet them. 'Acquisition', 'utilization', 'improvemental' and 'retention' show the wide scope of manpower planning. The subject suggests a subject concerned with a developing range of manpower policies, including those for recruitment, deployment, development and retention.

In fact, the concept of manpower planning is still in the process of evolution. It can not be treated as being absolute process of evolution. It can not be treated as being absolute and rigid. The ambit of manpower planning has enlarged with the passage of time and these days the concept has become so wide that includes almost every aspect of development economic and social. In the words of Professor Harbison, "In the broadest terms manpower policy should be concerned with development, maintenance and utilization of actual or potential members of labour force, including, those who are fully and productively employed as well as those who in getting work. The development of manpower is the process of man's acquiring the skills, knowledge and capacities for work... . The maintenance of manpower is the process of preservation and continuous renewal of man's capacities for work. The utilization of man power is the process of matching men and work in accordance with their level or development.... Thus, a comprehensive manpower policy would encompass as programmes of activities along these lines.

In its economic sense manpower planning includes the development and effective utilization of the managerial, scientific, engineering, technical and other skills which are used for creating, designing and developing organizations, managing and operating productive services, enterprises and economic institutions. Manpower Planning as a part of an integrated plan for economic development of a country must necessarily be related to the economic goals to be achieved and the nature of a economy to be established. Manpower planning should also include labour force mobility, migration, flexibility of workers, health requirements and consequently, a whole range of institutions. As such the concept of manpower planning must change with each stage of development of the economy. It should also be pointed out that manpower planning can not be independent. It must necessarily be a part of the general plan of economic development.

Manpower Planning and Economic Development

Manpower planning is an integral part of economic planning. There is also close coordination between economic development and manpower planning, particularly in the three areas:

1. Technique/technological change
2. Structural change, and
3. Social change

In all the available literature of development it is stated that technological change is a prerequisite for the development of an underdeveloped economy. With the change in technique/technology it is argued that level of production will also increase. Further, adoption of any technology will be determined by the policies of concerned economy, size of labour force and its capacity to install it. In the early stages of development labour intensive techniques are usually suggested due to scarcity of capital and abundant labour. The basic idea behind this developments strategy is that not only output but employment also should increase over the period. Thus, with the technological change, simultaneously there is an increase in output, national income, per capita income etc., which finally increases the standard of living of population. With changes in techniques-technologies there will be demand for change in skills compound for which long term planning is essential. This will come under the jurisdiction of manpower planning.

During the phases of development structural changes are inevitable. In the early stages of development an economy is primarily agrarian, where agriculture is the main activity with low per capita income. As the development process goes on there is a shift from agriculture to industry with new sets of technologies. In this process there will be change in the skill requirements, because skills required in agricultural activities are different from those required for industrial activities. Thus, if an economy makes plans to change its present structure at the same time it has to make plan for the skill development which will be required in this process.

With the change in activity and techniques production increases which leads to rise in per capita income. Here structural and technological change which involves geographic occupational and industrial mobility necessitates social change in the formation of new institutions, values, and incentives social change entails cultural migration i.e. the move from a traditional to a modern, industrial culture and so on. The demands made by social change may well be more important than the demands made by the need for new skills.

Development planning and manpower planning are closely interlinked. This can be seen in the figure.

The Elements of Manpower Planning

There is no consensus of opinions regarding the methods of manpower planning. It is however certain that methods and techniques of manpower planning vary from countrý to country and will depend on the extent of resources (both physical and capital) available at a particular time.

There are four main elements of manpower planning which are as following:

1. Manpower Requirements : It is important element of manpower planning. To asses the manpower requirements future goals of economic planning should be clearly fined. To achieve

Relation between Development Planning and Manpower Planning

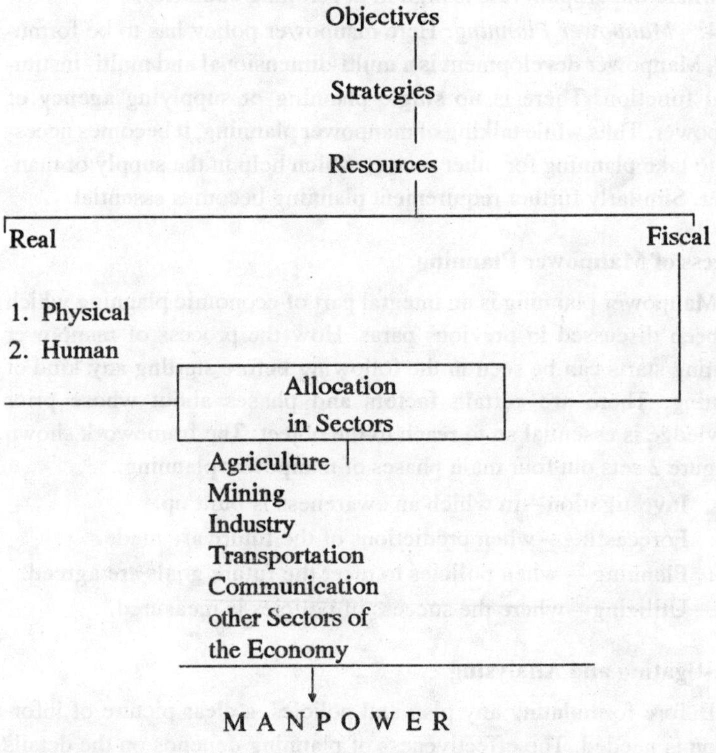

goals it becomes imperative to know that what type of resources are available, what will be the level and pattern of occupations, what should be the level of health, education, training and labour mobility required in future.

2. *Manpower Supply:* Assess the capacity of present system to meet these requirements that whether it is efficient to supply the required manpower. For example, if the number of engineers is a function of university engineering faculties, then the ability of the present system to produce an adequate number of engineers of a prescribed quality must be examined. If the present system is adjudged inadequate, changes must be envisaged.

3. *Institutional Planning:* Plan the institutions that supply manpower. The criteria should be manpoer requirements and efficiency. There is significant waste, especially in early primary educational system where the dropout rate is high in developing countries.

4. *Manpower Planning:* Here manpower policy has to be formulated. Manpower development is a multi-dimensional and multi- institutional function. There is no single planning or supplying agency of manpower. Thus while talking of manpower planning, it becomes necessary to take planning for other sectors which help in the supply of manpower. Similarly further requirement planning becomes essential.

Process of Manpower Planning

Manpower planning is an integral part of economic planning which has been discussed in previous paras. How the process of manpower planning starts can be seen in the following before starting any kind of planning. There are certain factors and phases about whose prior knowledge is essential so to reach to the object. The framework shown in Figure 2 sets out four main phases of manpower planning.

1. Investigation—in which an awareness is built up.
2. Forecasting—when predictions of the future are made.
3. Planning— when policies to meet the future goals are agreed.
4. Utilizing—where the success of policies is measured.

Investigating and Analysing

Before formulating any plan and policies, a clear picture of information is needed. The effectiveness of planning depends on the details and accuracy of the information on which it is based. Any failure to understand the problem at this stage may weaken the whole planning process.

Finance plays a crucial role in the development of any resource and similarly for the manpower development. In the process of manpower planning this knowledge of the financial accepts, will show that how much is being invested in the human resource development, are the present finances sufficient to meet the future tools, policies of the government regarding finances etc.

The analysis of productivity, practices and methods has organisational and individual aspect. The organization may have a particular methods of working and if this is changed to increase the production, there will be effect on manpower also. Thus knowledge of this aspect is to be taken for consideration before planning.

The study of external environments and its effects on general plan are quite common. Elements of external environment in this figure are external laboure supply, i.e., pattern of growth of population and labour force. Government policy towards it and education trends etc. Knowledge of all these aspects is essential for manpower planning.

The knowledge gleaned in the internal manpower review is particularly important to manpower planning. Here the main focus is on the opportunities inherent in the manpower employed. Analysis will be intended to highlight problems arising from the structure of the work force: for instance where technology has overtaken the skills available amongst employees to exploit it, or where the growth of one departmental activity and the decline of another is not reflected in organizational terms. Apart from structural problems there will be a need to look at the employees themselves regarding their age, skills, promotion etc.

Forecasting

Having a knowledge of all aspects of the economy, it is possible to move to attempts to indicate in which direction manpower is going to meet the objectives. The forecasting process throws up problems that may emerge. Forecasting has to be made both for manpower requirements and manpower supply. Manpower requirements mean demand for manpower. After the first phase i.e., investigation, it becomes easy to identify the nature of demand for a manpower for a given work load. Many things have to be kept in mind before forecasting demand for manpower. Prominent among these are the pattern of growth of an organization policies regarding services of employees, role of government either in promotion or demotion, market pattern etc. If all are in four these will definitely influence the nature and extent of demand for manpower. On the other hand supply of manpower is a function of present and expected labour force, level of education, skills which virtually determines the supply side.

Having assessed the levels of demand and supply of manpower, planner's attention turns towards the plans and policies needed to ensure that intention is translated into practice. The purpose of planning is to formulate coherent and interrelated policies designed to achieve the organization's manpower objectives. The policies regarding recruitment and training should be of such type which may help in the development of employees and which may help in making mutual relation between employees and employers. Similarly there should be advance planning keeping in view retirement, redundancy, industrial relations, transfers etc.

In the policies programmes are not implemented and better manpower utilization is not resulted the whole effort of manpower planning will be of little relevance. Hence there should be the effective implementation of policies. Effective implementation depends on the level of determination of existing manpower. Thus, throughout this description of manpower planning process the emphasis has been on flexibility and the flow of information from one phase to another. This interrelationship is important. It is perfectly feasible to undertake a manpower exercise such as wastage in isolation but if problems that emerge are to be solved it is inevitable that other factors become involved. For example, an analysis of a high labour turnover problem may highlisht overmanning (perhaps the employees are bored with having insufficient interesting work to occupy them) or undermanning. The organization is viewed as a system where action in one area has an effect elsewhere. This is why recruitment and training decisions cannot be dealt with separately, the implementation of one leading to the need of other.

Thus, it is evident from the above concepts of poverty, unemployment, and manpower planning that how important are these concepts in the literature of development economics. Though these three aspects are not directly interrelated but positively are interrelated indirectly. It is a general conception that with the unemployment there will be always poverty. But this concept was argued by Raj Krishna by saying that it is not necessary that poverty is the consequent of unemploymnt. Poverty has been identified not only with inequality but also with unemployment. Dandekar and Rath (1971) have defined as adequate level of employment in terms of it is capacity to provide minimum living to the population''. In his fourfold classification of unemployment Raj Krishna (1973) identifies this approach to unemployment as "the income criterion". It has been also observed in various studies that through proper manpower planning how effectively unemployment can be eradicated. By booking into the nature of demand and supply of manpower through a proper manpower planning, structural regional and sectoral imbalances can be bridged up. To know about the one concept it become

imperative to know about the other two also.

Notes and References

1. A.K. Sen, "Poverty, Inequality and Unemployment: Some Conceptual Issues in Measurements"' in Poverty and Income Distribution in India, Edited by T.N. Srinivasan and P.K. Bardhan, 1974, pp. 67- 68.
2. Poverty in terms of inequality has been defined in Ojha and Bhatt (1963), Victor Fuchs (1967) and B. Kumar (1977). Barbara Ward in his preface to Mahbub U Haq's: Poverty Curtain—The Choices of the Third World: considers the poorest as the bottom 20 or 30 per cent of the population. For a concept in poverty in terms of nutritional deficiency see Rowntree (1899), P.D. Ojha (1969), Dandekar and Rath (1971), Desai et al (1976) and Kalirajan (1976). The poverty line approach is used widely. All poverty debates in India make use of this concept. For deficiency of basic minimum needs, see Gadgil (1965). For the concept of poverty in terms of insufficiency of income to meet socially (or otherwise) accepted minimum needs see Dorthy Wedderburn (1974).
3. B. S Rowntree, "Poverty—A Study of Life", 1922, quoted in A.B. Athinson. The Economic of Inequality, p. 126.
4. Peter Townsend, (ed.) "The Concept of Poverty", 1970, pp., 2, 19, 42.
5. Martin Rein, "Problems in the Definition and Measurement of Poverty''.
6. Dorthy Wedderburn (ed), "Poverty, Inequality and Class Structure', 1974, pp. 15-16.
7. ***Ibid.***
8. V.G. Rao and G.P. Misra, (ed). "Rural Poverty: Growth and Determinate" in Employment, Poverty and Public Policy, 1981, pp. 204- 205.
9. **Ibid.**
10. I.Z. Bhatty, "Inequality and Poverty in Rural India," in T.N. Srinivasan and P.K. Bardhan eds., Poverty and Income Distribution in India, 1974, p. 292.
11. Micheal Rose, E., "The Relief of Poverty: 1834-1914; 1972, pp. 6.
12. Charles Booth, "Labour and Life of the People in London" (1902). Some chapters dealing with East London were printed in 1989, reprinted in 1969.
13. N. Gopalda, "Unemployment and Employment Planning," Calcutta, 1968, p. 7.
14. Priyendra Bahadur, "The Concept of Disguised Unemployment Reconsidered", Indian Journal of Labour Economics, Vol. III, 1960-61, p. 76.
15. Report of the Ninth International Conference of Labour Statisticians, I.L.O., Geneva.
16. Johan Robinson, "Essays in the Theory of Employment", 1947, p. 84 and Disguised Unemployment, "Economic Journal, Vol. 46, June, 1936, p. 226.

17. W. Arthur Lewis, "Economic Development with Unlimited Supply of Labour, see Reading in Economic Development, Edited by Morgan, T. and others, 1963; W.A. Lewis, the Theory of Economic Growth, Homewood, 1955, p. 326.
18. Keynes meaning of equilibrium was perhaps different from classicists because:
    (i) his was not a general equilibrium,
    (ii) his was a short-run analysis only.
19. R.K. Srivastava, "Projecting Manpower Demand—A Review of Methodology", 1964. Directorate of Manpower, Ministry of Home Affairs, Govt. of India.
20. A Manpower Programme for Economic Development, Ministry of Home Affairs, Government of India, Dec., 1960, p.1.
21. HMSO, Company Manpower Planning, 1974.
22. "Towards Manpower Policy", ed. by R.A. Gordon John Wilay and Sons, Inc, New York, 1967 pp. 136-38.
23. Dandekar and Rath, **op. cit.**
24. Raj Krishna.

5

Whither Democratic Planning—An Utopia on Integrated Planning

N. SHRIDHARAN

Day in and out, in the Ratio, TV and in the News paper, in the street corners, every where, the slogan "Garibi Hatao" rings in our ears and dilutes in our dolorous memories. The First Five Year Plan started this slogan and even the discussion papers on the Eighth Plan repeats the same chime. We are not at all ashamed to repeat this slogan even after 37 years of planned development. Where we are going wrong? Are our policies on 'democratic socialism' weakening? Or the newly rich dominates the country's future? Or the continuous persistence of terrorism weakend our political thinking capacity? Though we got the freedom forty years ago, we fixed the freedom fighters on the wall and in the street corners to be remembered only on Independence Days and Republic Days, without even recollecting the values imparted by them. We do not have even that much of patriotism for our country which the people of those countries which got freedom centuries before us has. We are consoled and convinced to identify ourselves with our castes, religion, language and the region rather than identifying ourselves as an Indian. How long this trend will go on? What does the socalled National Integration Council and the All-India parties doing?

The Colonial government was interested in the policy of divide and rule so as to safeguard their interest. We bequeathen the same policy and adopting it even now in many form to safeguard the interests of vested groups. Any layman who scans through the pages of the Five Year Plans, will be taken aback after seeing the crores and crores of money spent on wasteful expenditures. Where and what returns these investments have made on the Indian economy, only a few knows, and that too the few segment of the population who were benefitted by the scheme (if at all these are any persons in this list). We are trumpeting boldly that we have one of the highest savings rate (26 per cent) in the World. Only God knows where these savings are diverted. We have too many things to learn from our immediate neighbour, China, particularly in the field of human resource development/manpower planning.

Under the veil of democracy and delineation of power, we have embarked upon a programme of creating too many agencies and Commissions at all levels — Centre, State, Local and even Village level — in order to give a helping hand to our beloved MLAs, M.Ps, and to retired judges to earn their bread. One wonders, whether any sort of integration exist among these commissions/agencies/boards. How can we even think of the 21st century when we haven't reached even the 19th century in terms of providing the basic needs? Is it the same vicious circle of poverty which the great economist Ragnar Nurkse thought of, is still gripping our economy? Are we not going to prove that our economy is no longer a developing economy but a developed one? If so, when? It is neither neo-classicalism, Keynesianism nor the Marxism going to cure our development efforts but a sincere dedication at all levels from the politician to ordinary lay man can cure our own problems. How to go about in solving this?

Solutions

Need for Policy Statements: First of all, we have to accept the truth that we lack policy statements on many important issues such as manpower planning, urban development, resource development, and other areas. Of late, new ministries are being formed for dealing with different types of problems faced by the government, which by itself is a welcoming trend. A proper and meaningful integration of various schemes/programmes formulated and implemented by these ministries at different levels will go a long way in finding solutions to our problems. The existing system of integration is so weak that there is no integration at all, at any level.

Curbing Wasteful Expenditure

A little more than 25 per cent of our country's expenditure goes into non-developmental expenditure. Let us analyse one example to show how our policies are going wrong and how much of money is being wasted. Let us start from the rural area and from the Integrated Rural Development Programme (IRDP), which the government claims to be a most successful one in reducing the rural poverty. This programme is supposed to be 'integrated' and this along with the Twenty Point Economic Programme aims at eliminating poverty from the rural scene. The programme identifies the poorest of the poor and gives him loan cum subsidy so as to enable him to earn enough regular income (His income is supposed to be high enough, to maintain the asset, to repay the loan from the bank alongwith interest, to bribe the people around so as to get his other obligations done and also to maintain his family with 2,400 calories of food intake every day), so that he comes out of the clutches, of poverty. Is it not too ambitious to plan like this, even at the micro level? How can any person who doesn't have any previous experience in selling goods and those who do not know about the diseases of the imported cow can maintain the business/cow and get as much income from the holy cow and survive? Are we are not cheating ourselves? Moreover the minimum wages fixed under the Minimum Wages Act keeps the agriculturist much below the poverty line. What kind in integration has been made and where?

Every year 600 families are identifies in each of the 5,000 odd block in our country and an amount of rupees hundred thousand are being spent per annum. Whose money is it any way? And in a country where in thee is an accute scarcity of capital, how many wonders this fifty crores can do? The only pride the politicians are getting is that of distributing the money to safeguard their vote banks in the rural area. The pertinent question that emerges is that, are we doing justice to the socalled 'Social Justice' by snatching away the hard earnest money from the middle income groups by way of direct and indirect taxes and spend the same in the rural area. The rich usually escapes any kind of tax impositions through their high level connections or through illegal means. It is not one or two years we thought about eradicating poverty, but ever since the First Five Year Plan, the foremost objective of our Plans remained the same. No doubt the recent statistics can prove the increase in the standard of living in the rural area but the same statistics can also prove the widening gap in the distribution of income within the rural area. Who has to be blamed for this condition? Are the planners (generally the blame takers) responsible or the administrators responsible or last but not least the poor people are responsible? It is very easy to shift the blame from one segment to the other segment of the population but the affected ones are the poor people who continues to remain in the veil of poverty for ever and ever. The blame lies with the politicians, administrators partially and on the other on people themselves.

The politicians take the sole privilage of decision-making and their decisions are governed by, infact decided by, the vested interest who provides all the infrastructural facilities including finance for election purposes. The planners, administrators have to take whatever is thrown at them by these powerful groups in the country. They implement all the schemes from rural development schemes to industrial development as per the interest of these groups. Within the ambit of these groups if a poor person comes he is really indeed very-very lucky. The poor has to be blamed at the outset, because he is the person who elects the politician. He is illiterate and poverty torn. These two chronic diseases make him blind when the money is pushed into his pocket to decide the political game. It is difficult for him to perceive the long term costs and benefits and at the same time he is worried about that day's food which is not there. Thus the so called 'Democratic Socialism' pushes him further down far away from democracy and far away from socialism. He is neither bothered about who rules him nor aware of any of the government programmes. The reasons are very clear. There is a deliberate communication gap created at different level by different people to safeguard their own interest. For example: More than 50 per cent of our villages are not connected by *pucca* road and those which are connected also becomes inaccessible for more than four months in a year due to active monsoon and subsequent submersion of these roads. How much true Michael Franda was when he wrote on his Indian experience, in the book "Small is Politics"? When the small itself is politics in India, there is no word to describe the monster.

Corrective Measures

"What corrective measures can be taken and at what level" Though a decision to this effect involves bold and sacrosant action, this is hard to come from a politician or from the Government officials or from the people themselves. The people should be prepared to work for their bread. The politicians should shed their power hungerness and more out with real decisions without getting impaired by the vested interest groups. The action called for is to be taken at the National level, presently at which most of the policy decisions are being taken. The actions to be taken are enumerated below.

Planning and Development of Human Resource : One of the greatest asset of our nation is the human resource. About 54 per cent of India's population is in the working age group of 15 to 59 years of age. In this there are about 30 million officially registered unemployed persons. So far we have not formulated any policy to utilise this huge amount of human resources directly. All our earlier policies have been indirectly aimed at employment generation as one of its aim. Even the recently formulated Ministry of Human Resource Development still think in terms of providing education to the rural and urban population and how to improve the skills of the teachers. This may solve the problem in future only and that too if a proper co-ordination takes place among various departments and the ministries. Why not the Ministry come out boldly on this issue? Let their be a policy which can say that those below secondary education should serve in the army compulsorily for a minimum period of ten years and those completed secondary education for five years and so on.

Needless to say about these who haven't stepped into the schools and about the dropouts. Even in the advanced countries such as USA, Germany this system exist, particularly for higher level posts in the government. When we can copy all the other things from the West, why not this too? What prevents us from doing this practice of compulsory military training? The much celebrated poverty alleviation programmes can be stopped and the amount spent on these can be used for this purpose. Tonnes of food surpluses gained can be used to feed this service population. Each and every individual from the politician to the pot maker in our country will accept the fact that the role of army is not for fighting the war alone but used for various constructive activities such as flood relief work, dam constructions, road buildings and the like. This compulsory military training can give the people free food a day and a place to reside. The services provided by these people can be utilised for those schemes which were hither too considered impossible by the Government. Their services can be used for afforestation work, laying roads to connect the villages, providing water supply.

It is not at all impossible to achieve all these infrastructural developments which are much needed, when it is possible for us go to Antartic, when it is possible to series of satellites when it is possible to supply gas from Arabic sea to a far of areas of U.P. This compulsory service in the army will also enable the people to come out of their narrow regional, linguistic, caste and clan feelings and may impart the feeling of national spirit. Definitely everyone will be proud to claim himself or herself as an Indian rather than a Bengali, Tamilian, Punjabi and so on. This compulsory service in the army will also solve the problem of unemployment and under-employment wide-spread in our economy. It will also enable our planners to assess the demand for various technical and non-technical skills and to forecast the requirements for the future. This will also increase the literacy rate in the country, may be out of fear initially. This policy can also stop to some extent or control to some extent the menacing growth of population. This policy involves neither changes in the system nor changes in the Government but just a change of heart of the decision makers at the top.

Nationalisation of Rivers

In India even a small pond is considered as holy and rituals are performed every year. People are ready to spend their life's savings to have a holy dip and darshan of Ganges and Jamuna and come all the way from the tip of the South to the Corner's of North India. The five perennial rivers overflow every year causing greatest damage to the people and to the crop. On the otherhand, there is an acute shortage of water resources in the South and in the West. Neither any perennial rivers passes through these States nor the rivers that flow there has adequate water for all seasons. River water being the State subject under the constitution, usually the concern States are not willing to share the river waters with the neighbouring States. Even after 30 years of planning only 27 per cent of the total agricultural area has been irrigated. Similarly, a considerable amount of money is spent every year on flood control and drought relief. Is it not possible to nationalise the rivers and link the northern rivers with the south rivers?

Why should not we think in term of long term planning of water resources? It is impossible to accept that there is not enough money or our country's geography won't allow this national linkages. It is possible to use the labour acquired through compulsory military training to implement this monstrous task. Let our granaries feed this labour force. Within a decade we can see the real development that is taking place in India. These changes in the policy involves no change in the system of planning nor it requires a separate commission. More dedication and bold decisions are involved leaving aside partisan attitude and catering the interested groups. This will bring prosperity and self-sufficiency to our lakhs of Indian villages than any rural development programme can directly bring about.

Privatisation of Public Sector — Cure or the Cause

The privatisation of public sector companies, a fever started in the western world recently and transmitted to our Indian sub-continent, is suppose to cure all the recent economic debacles of our country. Given the twin goals of Equity and Efficiency enshrined in our constitution, is it not idealistic to talk about privatisation? In a country where corruption and laziness are the twin goals of the people how the twin goals of constitution can be fulfilled? The major public sector industries which are running under accumulated losses should be given to private sector for few years, say for five to ten years.

Definitely the private managers will weed out those in efficient and non-dynamic element from these white elephants. Public sector has to benefit all the people and not to the section of the people who have vested interest in their operation. It is impossible to allow, in the name of 'democratic socialism or socialistic pattern', any one to ruin and squander the wealth of our country. Otherwise the public sector should be made responsible for the losses incurred by it by making the head of the organisation individually responsible for this.

It is illogical to argue that coal mines, iron industries and other big industries are very much needed for the upliftment of the poor, so all these will have to be under public sector only. On the other hand, these heavy industries do have an important role to play in the development of our economy. So for these heavy industries have not created any trickle down effect. If any one argues that it is only due to these industries that development has taken place, why don't they explain, why Bihar and West Bengal which were industrialised early 30s, ranks high even today in terms of people living below poverty. The only way these imbalances can be explained is that of improper and inadequate information system combined with very low provision of infrastructural facilities. Even if the private entrepreneurs who comes out boldly to set up industries in the most backward areas are often discouraged by the inadequate facilities and too many formalities. To a great extent we all can agree that there is a misconception on priority. Misconception in the sense, the government does not know what is more important to eradicate poverty first or to go in for prestigious schemes such as Asiad and the World Cups. To spend crores and crores of rupees every year on flood relief and drought relief works or to go in for well planned national irrigation network. To spend huge money every year under the banner of rural upliftment or to go in for real infrastructural development in the rural areas. Is it not true that we are being misguided and we are going on the wrong path in the process of development. Development is being eluded away from us.

Who is the culprit? Every individual is a culprit including myself. Because we neither have an ambition for our Nation's development nor we have even a bit of patriotism for our country.

A compulsory training in the army coupled with a proper, well planned long term manpower policy alongwith dedication at all level will eradicate poverty rather than spending crores of rupees on the short-term money oriented solutions. We have to decide, are we going to march ahead with this idea of development to the 21st century, or, to carry alongwith us the same old ideas and techniques combined with corruption self-interest to the 21st century? The option is wide open to us.

6

Regional Disparities in Demographic Development

K.N. DUBEY

Introduction

The base objective of development is the improvement of quality of life of the people in all the areas. In fifty's and early sixty's ideas of economic determinism was too strong. Prevailing notion of the time was that if economic growth, especially GRD (Gross Domestic Product) was taken care that would automatically take care of other aspects. Subsequently substantial economic progress and development took place. Especially in Third World Countries development was also accompanied by poverty, illiteracy, malnutrition, hunger, structural inequality and regional disparities. All this made the early notion untenable. In the development process large section of the population was left behind. Development became lopsided. The gap between rich and poor people and between rich and poor areas remained high. In some cases the gap was further widened. (See Misra et al. 1974; Bhat et al. 1982; Misra et al., 1985).

Due to this a new thinking started gaining momentum. This is along with development direct measures for the improvement of quality of life is essential (Seer, 1969; ILO, 1977: Gosal and Krishan, 1984; Singh and Dubey, 1985). Reasoning behind this change in development thinking is simple. The people have double role in the process of development. On one hand they are factor of production as work force and effective market for goods and services. On the other people are sole beneficiary of the entire process of development. Therefore all development should address the people. Increase in welfare and improvement in quality of life of the people should be the main concern of the development.

In India since independence people's welfare and development has acquired high attention. Gandhian concept of Achhutodihar (upliftment of untouchables) and Mahilothan (upliftment of women), Nehruvian Concept of wiping the tears from every eyes, and Jayaprakash Narayan's concept of Sarvodaya (upliftment of all) are clear evidence. Constitution of India lays down the provisions of universal literacy, health services and rise in the level of nutrition and standard of living of the people (Article 47). In planning and development process initiation of people welfare programmes, adoption of Target Group Oriented Development Approach Minimum Needs Programme. Direct assault on poverty and recent formulation of Ministry of Human Resource Development have been the significant steps in this direction. Even the process of people's development was slow and uneven.

Literacy, an essential element for good quality of life, was 16.67 per cent in 1951, remained 24.02 per cent in 1961, slowly picked up to 29.46 per cent in 1971 and 36.23 per cent in 1981. The urban male non-scheduled castes literacy (67.99 per cent) was almost eight times higher to that of rural female scheduled castes (8.45 per cent) in 1981. Urban literacy (57.40 per cent) was almost double to rural literacy (29.68 per cent). In the same way male literacy (46.89 per cent) and non-scheduled castes literacy position (39.01 per cent) was for better in comparison to that of scheduled castes (21.38 per cent) and scheduled tribes (21.38 per cent) Dubey 1989, 26.

In the country five districts were urban. In just contract ten districts were rural devoid of urban population. Kerala state, not a very rich state even on Indian standard, with 23.3 per thousand birth rates and 6.8 per thousand death rates (1985) attained demographic transition. Contrastingly Haryana one of the developed states with 33.0 birth rates and 10.8 death rates was far behind on the scale of demographic transition. The position of Bihar, Madhya Pradesh and Uttar Pradesh were more disappointing. The present paper is an endeavour to analyze these intricacies. It attempts to visualize regional disparities in demographic development and suggests remedies for the removal of those disparities.

The paper starts with reassertion of two seminal hypotheses: one by Raza and another by Bose. Raza (1978) postulated that regional pattern of development in India consisted of a hungry belly most extensive in Central India and relatively developed periphery. His unit of observation. He characterized central part of India consisting of Bihar, Madhya Pradesh, Rajasthan and Uttar Pradesh as BIMARU. (Sick) states. His observation was based on demographic behaviour of these states.

In the light of above two statements the present paper starts with two basic premises. First, in analysis of regional disparities units of investigation should be as homogeneous as possible and practicable. The NSS Regions and more so the states are too large and too diverse units. In other words intra unit diversities are not less pronounced than the inter unit diversities. This study adopts district as unit of investigation which has been acclaimed as most effective unit to represent the grass-roots realities (Dubey and Singh 1990; Krishan 1984; Planning Commission, 1984).

Secondly Raza employed a volley of 102 indicators of development representing all possible gamut of development. But Bose made his observation primarily on the basis of two elements of demography: fertility and mortality. The present study is limited to demographic development. It takes a comprehensive view of demographic development. In consonant with the basic premise remaining part of the paper is organized in order of a conceptual, analytical and synthesis sequence.

Conceptual Framework and Methodology

Despite a long realization of demographic development the concept of demographic development is vague. What is demographic development? No direct answer is available in the existing literature. A large number of books bearing little demography are of no help (Pressat, 1969; Dyson and Crook (1984); CDP Report, 1988; Jayagopal 1990). A perusal of studies employing demographic indicators may throw some light on this issue. Schwartezberg (1962) in his study on regional variations in economic development in India used seven demographic indicators: proportion of urban population, share of urban population in towns having population of one lakh plus, proportion of non-agricultural workers and factory workers per lakh population. His focus was on urbanization and diversification of economy. He did not include the indicators of physical quality of life like literacy.

Social Statistics Division of United Nations (1977) identified sixteen demographic indicators and grouped them into four categories: population stock, births, deaths and migration. Some additional demographic indicators were also listed under other categories and subcategories. The underlying idea was that demographic. However in traditional high population zone, where acute population pressure is demurring, population stock is hardly an index of development.

Rao (1977) suggested six demographic indicators to discern the stage of socio-economic development; growth rate, birth rate, death rate, general fertility rate, net rural urban migration rate and percentage of urban population. His focus was on different elements of population dynamics as representative of development level. A major point of caution in this case would be to interpret a given population dynamics only in the context of total situation of an area, for instance rural-urban migration may suggest a high employment potential of towns. But in reality it may be the consequence of rural impoverishment as is the case in many of the densely populated developed countries.

By using the Indian Census data, Harvey and Bhardwaj (1973) worked out fourteen indices to represent socio-economic aspects of modernization, indices of non-subsistence, traditional crafts, primary employment, range of commerce, literacy, female literacy, circulation, migration dependency and scheduled castes component among those were strictly demographic in nature.

Gosal and Krishan (1984) were pioneer to examine the demographic aspect of development. The employed fourteen indicators: One pertaining to urbanization, four to literacy and nine to occupational structure. The authors, however, did not offer any definition of demographic development. They also did not explain why only one indicator of urbanization and as much as nine indicators of occupational structure were included.

Morris applied Physical Quality of Life Index (PQLI) based on three demographic index of infant mortality rate, life expectany at age one and adult literacy age fifteen and over. This is a good index for the measurement of the performance of poor countries in meeting in the most basic human needs. To adopt it as measure of demographic development would be reduction of the concept of demographic development which is much broader than the literacy, reduction of infant mortality and increase of life expectancy. Apart from conceptual limitation the micro level available data on infant mortality and life expectancy in India are highly unreliable. Hence these indicators are not practicable (Dube, 1984).

The above review does not lead us to any clear cut concept of demographic development. Scholars, barring a few exceptions, used demographic attributes as indicators of economic and social development rather of demographic development. Theoretically a definition of demographic development must encompass the spirit of both demography and development. Accordingly it may be defined as the demographic performance of an area in terms of pattern of life, as reflected in urban-rural component, quality of life as manifested in its literacy rates and level of economic dynamism as suggested by its occupational structure.

Increase of urbanization is a clear gain for attitudinal change. It inculcates new values and progressive attitudes which lessen the rigorous of conservatism in general and caste barriers in particular (Haselitz; 1975, 160-62). A hierarchy of urban centres work as a channel for trickle down of urban impulses in rural areas. Urbanization reduces the pressure of people on agricultural land and provides more remunerative jobs without decreasing the production in agricultural sector. Therefore urbanization should be visualized as urban development in terms of degree of urbanization, effectiveness of urbanization and service component of urban centres to rural population and to rural areas.

The development of literacy is of utmost significance in underdeveloped areas. It is an investment in human capital. In the areas where development has not progressed very for and literacy is low, the marginal gains from education and training are high (Chisholm, 1982, 49). Literacy is instrumental in increase of skill, eradication of ignorance and in establishment of social justice. It is important in case of females and scheduled castes who remained the real dreg of society. The female literacy is counted as the best contraceptive as the literate and educated women are more responsive to family planning measures.

The most important dimension of demographic development is the structural transformation of working force. In India the distribution of working force is highly skewed in favour of agricultural sector since three-fourth population is in agricultural sector. Thereby three farm families are feeding one non-farm family. And one non-farm family is providing the other needs of three farm families. This retarded the whole process of economic development. Clark (1957) observed the importance of shift of resources including population from primary sector to manufacturing and service sectors. The plausible reason is increasing return in manufacturing in contrast to supposed diminishing return in agriculture. To represent there intricacies of demographic development the indicators were developed as given in Table 6.1.

In a highly dense populated area one like India increase in the quality of human life is a distinct gain in the demographic development. But increase in absolute number may be hardly a benefit. In acute poverty condition children are used for the minor jobs. But that is hardly a sign of development. In such areas decline in birth and death rates and increase in life expectancy would be strong indicators of development. Data on these counts at grass-roots level are not available and these indicators could not be included. But urbanization, literacy and occupational structure would take full care of physical quality of life.

Theoretically each indicator included in the measurement of demographic development is significant. Therefore it would be appropriate to measure regional disparities in respect of each indicator. The absolute disparities on those indicators may be discerned by substracing the value of bottom position unit from the value of top position unit. But in Indian condition where exceptions are rural, jumping and sinking of values are usual. As such range of top and bottom ranking units would provide a distorted figure. Therefore disparity index was calculated by:

Value of top position unit minus value of bottom position unit divided by value of mediam position unit.

India: Indicators of Demographic Development

1. Urban population as per cent of total population.
2. Population in 20,000+ towns as per cent of total population.
3. Number of towns per lakh of rural population.
4. Number of towns per thousand square kilometers of rural area.
5. Literates as per cent of total population.
6. Literate females as per cent of total female population.
7. Rural literates as per cent of total rural population.
8. Scheduled Caste literates as per cent of Scheduled Caste population.
9. Workers in non-agricultural activities as per cent of total main workers.
10. Rural workers in non-agricultural activities as per cent of total rural main workers.
11. Workers in household industry, manufacturing, processing servicing and repairs as per cent of total main workers.
12. Other workers as per cent of total main workers.

This index takes care of excessive distortion. At the same it does not eliminate altogether impact of jumping and sinking which are a part of grassroots reality.

Analysis

In India the regional disparities in various dimensions of demographic development were very high. It was highest in urban development followed by in occupational dynamism and literacy development.

Within urban development disparity was highest in case of urban efficiency (10.23) represented by proportion of urban population in living 20000 + towns to total population. But it was relatively low in case of urbanization (6.36). Disparity was further high in regard to sufficiency of towns in terms of rural population (7.7). It was too high in case of accessibility of towns in terms of rural areas (121.20).

Like urban development degree of disparity varied in literacy rate of different socio-economic groups. It was higher in case of weaker sections of population like scheduled castes (4.78), females (3.95) and rural population (2.78). High disparity of scheduled castes literacy needed some in depth probe. A few districts in Jammu and Kashmir where scheduled castes population was negligible and consisted of mostly migrant one had very high scheduled castes literacy rate. This exceptional high literacy rate inflated the degree of disparity in scheduled castes literacy. High disparity in weaker section population further aggravated their low position.

Disparity in case of occupational position stood in between the disparity in urban and in literacy development. Again it was relatively low in case of diversification of total main workers (3.51) than in case of total main worker in rural areas (3.98). It is very high in case of household workers (7.51) followed by other workers (3.98).

Not only disparity was high at macro national level but also at meso state level. Table 6.2 presents of degree of disparity in select components of demographic development within the states. In urbanization micro state like Sikkim (9.81) and major states namely Andhra Pradesh (8.42), West Bengal (6.76), Bihar (5.97) and Madhya Pradesh (5.23) have more than or equal to all India disparities within the state. Similar position was in case of literacy and occupational dynamism measured by proportion of workers is non-agricultural activities to total main workers.

Table 6.2
Indian Pattern of Disparity in Select Component of Demographic Development, 1981

State		Urbanization	Literacy	Diversification of workers
1.	Andhra Pradesh	8.42	1.33	2.97
2.	Bihar	5.97	0.85	3.35
3.	Gujarat	2.75	0.78	1.58
4.	Haryana	1.52	0.53	1.59
5.	Himachal Pradesh	2.23	0.66	0.99
6.	Jammu and Kashmir		1.32	1.92
7.	Karnataka	2.23	0.75	1.69
8.	Kerala	3.00	0.37	1.03
9.	Madhya Pradesh	5.23	1.47	3.00
10.	Maharashtra	4.25	0.89	3.44
11.	Manipur	4.15	0.31	2.44
12.	Meghalaya	3.09	0.62	3.43
13.	Nagaland	2.42	0.94	1.29
14.	Orissa	2.46	0.97	1.18
15.	Punjab	1.20	0.56	0.67
16.	Rajasthan	1.12	1.05	1.08
17.	Sikkim	9.81	0.63	1.48
18.	Tamil Nadu	3.46	0.83	2.32
19.	Tripura	1.15	0.26	0.51
20.	Uttar Pradesh	3.72	1.34	2.53
21.	West Bengal	6.76	1.25	2.54
INDIA		6.36	2.35	3.51

Pattern of Demographic Development

Map 1 present the spatial pattern of demographic development that reveals distressing position in most of the areas. Only exceptions are one high and a few peaks associated with high development and a few trench and deeps associated with enervating ecological and demographic development is conspicuous. Here a long tradition of high literacy interconnected with Christian traditions and Christian missionary activities, plantation, agriculture, continuous series of settlement pattern and overall welfare activities initiated by leftist state government have positive impact on development of the people.

Apart from the high land of demographic development erstwhile colonial enclaves of port towns namely Bombay, Calcutta, Haora, Ahmedabad, Madras, Pondichery, Yemen, Mahe, Goa, Daman and Diu and a few administrative towns like Nation capital New Delhi and State capitals Hyderabad, Gandhinagar, Bhopal, and Srinagar raised the status of their respective districts in demographic development.

In just contrast to scatted high and peaks of demographic development, trench and deeps of demographic distress are more pronounced and highly contiguous. The most extensive trenches are associated with two physical ecological conditions and two with tribal ecology. Out of two physical ecological trenches one in cotermiuns with Terai belt in the state of Uttar Pradesh and Bihar. The Gorakhpur district divides this belt into two equal halves: western and eastern. This trench starts from Kheri district and incorporating Bahraich, Gonda, Barabanki, Deoria, Siwan, Gopalganj, Paschim Champaram, Purba Champaram, Sitamarhi, Makhubani, Sabarsa, Purnia reached upto Katihar in the east. The one arm of this trench passing through poverty through Uttar Pradesh reaches upto Panna district in Madhya Pradesh. In this areas ecological condition of enervating *Terai* hindered the process of demographic development. Its south world extending areas is associated with submergence of development impulses coming from the west and good physical conditions moving from east to west direction.

Apart from this extensive trench of demographic distress four other wide demographic deeps are much pronounced. One is associated with desert ecology located at Indo-Pak border in Thar desert covering the district of Barmer and Jolor in Rajasthan. The remaining three deeps are associated with cultural ecology. Among them the most extensive is Madhya Pradesh, Orissa and Andhra Pradesh counterminus with the district of Bastar, Koraput and Kalahandi. Second one is on Bihar and Madhya Pradesh border in the districts of Sidhi, Sarguja and Palamau. Lastly third one is on Madhya Pradesh and Rajasthan border comprising the districts of Dhar, Jhabua and Banswara.

With the exceptions of above high peaks and trench and deeps of demographic development a girdle of low demographic plain starting form Ludhiana in the west covering whole of Rajasthan desert, incorporating Vindhyachal mountain, Kaimur range, submerges in the demographic trench of Terai in north Bihar. This girdle divides India into two parts: India of inside the girdle and India on outside of the girdle. The inside girdle covers most of the north India plain. In this part level of demographic development decreases from west to east. Obviously it follows the direction of green revolution impulse that decreases from west to east. It has inverse auto correlation with the amount of average annual rainfall that increases from east to west. Again it has inverse association with erstwhile colonial penetration and influence, the diffusion which spread from east to west direction.

In just contrast out side of the dividing girdle that extends in peninsular south Indian demographic development decreases from coastal area to interior part of the country. In general the direction of demographic development is in conformity with east while colonial influence in the southern India.

The most conspicuous feature of demographic development in India is that unlike other countries of the world southern India is relatively at higher demographic development plain than the north India. It is significant that tropical climatic conditions are more enervating in the south than in the north India. Meaning by that the most part of the country has attained the state where physical factors in the determination of demographic performance of the area are relatively less significant than the socio-economic and cultural factors.

The grass-roots spatial realities of demographic developments falsify the concept of 'hungry belly' in central India. At the same spatial structure of demographic development in all the states is highly variable. Hence the concept of Bimaru states of Bose is over generalization of the reality.

One important feature so called Bimaru states of India is extensive stretches of demographic trench and deeps associated with physical and tribal ecology. That dragged the state average position downward. On the other end of spectrum Bhopal and Indore in Madhya Pradesh; and Dhanbad in Bihar are among the peaks of demographic development. Western part of Uttar Pradesh and whole of Uttar Pradesh mountain are at par with the developed region of India. Hence it would be plausible to state that there are no *Bimaru States* in India. Only a few *Bimaru* (Sick) tracts exist. The areas designated demographic trench and deeps those *Bimaru* tracts.

Policy Option

In India the grass-roots demographic development conditions do not conform national or state average position. The policy formulation on the meso and micro basis would be far from grass-roots realities. This reasserts the need or decentralization of planning process at grass-roots level. This will bring the input of local wisdom for the removal of local demographic development hindrances.

Secondly at least four types of demographic development areas are easily discernible. One the tracts of demographic trench and deeps that could not absolve from their physical and cultural ecological constraints. Such tracts are economic as well as demographic distress zones. These are the real sick tracts and need greater care like a sick person. Effective answer to their problems would be big push and around development. The second is the peaks of demographic development associated with urbanization and large concentration of people. Here beneath the glittering urban civilization increasing slums, pollution and conservation are not less problematic.

The third type of area is the high plain of demographic development. In this area economic development is relatively ahead to demographic development. In this area direct measures for the improvement in quality of life of the people are required. Fourth one is the area of low plain of demographic development. Such areas are highly extensive and comprise highly density populated tracts of east Uttar Pradesh, Bihar and West Bengal; moderately, populated tract of Deccan plateau; and low density populated tracts of Rajasthan desert and Uttara Khand mountainous zone. What is common in these tracts? Answer is acute poverty. Hence the direct assault on poverty is first and foremost prerequisite for the demographic development in areas.

Finally whether Kerala, the state of high demographic development, may be a model for demographic development in other parts of the country? The answer is not positive. The history, culture and settlement pattern of Kerala state are specific and unique. These characteristics are non-existing in other parts of the country. Hence area specific indigenous strategy for demographic development is the need of the time.

Notes and References

1. Structural inequality has been used in reference to uneven position among different socio-economic groups living in the same area. In contrast the term regional disparities is used in reference to the variation of position of one socio-economic group across the spatial units like state and districts.
2. Target Groups: Assistance is given to the rural families of target group having annual income below the cut-off line of Rs. 4,8000. The poverty line income is identified at Rs. 6,400. The target group includes small and marginal farmers, agricultural labourers and rural artisans. At least 30 per cent of the assisted are scheduled castes and scheduled tribes. Now it has been decided that 30 per cent assisted should be women. (Department of Rural Development, Government of India, Annual Report 1989-90 p. 21).
3. Minimum Needs Programmes is an integrated package programme initiated since Fifth Five Year Plan (1974-79). The programmes includes: (i) elementary education, (ii) adult education, (iii) rural water supply, (iv) rural roads, (v) rural electrification, (vi) house sites/houses for landless labourers, (vii) environmental improvement of slums, and (viii) nutrition. The programme is the expression of the commitment of the Government for the social and economic development of the community, particularly the undeserved and under privileged segment of population (Mazumdar and Wasan).
4. Demographic Transition Theory was postulated by Thompson (1929) and Notestein (1945). The theory postulates that demographic transformation of society moves together. This progress from high fertility, high mortality, highly urban, industrial and universal literacy stage.
5. National Sample Survey Organization divides the country into 56 units. On average one unit comprised 7.36 districts in 1981. (Based on NSS. 1971).
6. In India there were 22 states in 1981. The largest state in population, Uttar Pradesh, with 110.86 million population was more than 350 times bigger to smallest State Sikkim which had only 0.31 million population.
7. Dubey (1981) discovered poverty through in Uttar Pradesh starting from Bahraich district on northern boundary of the state covering Barabanki, Faizabd, Sultanpur, Pratapgarh, Raebarely, Fatehpur and Banda district on the southern boundary. It is a zone of sub-margins of natural impulses of development coming from the east and man made impulses of development from the west.

Bhat, L.S. et al (eds) (1982), Regional Inequalities in India: An Inter state and Intra-state Analysis, Society for the study of Regional Disparities, New Delhi.

Bose, A. (1988), Form Population to People, B.R. Publishing

Corporation, Delhi.

C.D.P. Report (1988), Human Resource Development: A Neglected Dimension of Developments Strategy, United Nation, New York.

Chisholm, M. (1982), Modern World Development: A Geographical Perspective, Hutchinson, London.

Clark, C. (1957), The Condition of Economic Growth, St. Martins, New York.

Dubey, K.N. and Singh, R.P.C. (1990) 'Centralized and Decentralized Planning in India: A Dialogue' in Dubey K.N. (ed.), Planning and Development in India, Ashish Publishing House, New Delhi.

Dubey, K.N. (1989), 'Geographic Background and Socio-Economic Development in India' in Madan, G.R. (ed.) Economic Problems in Modern India; Problems of Development, Allied Publishers, New Delhi.

Dubey, K.N. (1984), 'Pattern of the Poverty in the Third World', The Avoid Journal of Social Sciences, 1, 57-68.

Dubey, K.N. (1981), Regional Disparities in the Levels of Socio-Economic Development in an Indian State: A Case Study of Uttar Pradesh, Department of Geography, Punjab University, Chandigarh.

Dyson, T. and Crook, N. (1984), India's Demography: Essays Contemporary Population', South Asian Publishers, New Delhi.

First Report of the Ninth Finance Commission (1989-90), Ministry of Finance, New Delhi.

Gosal, G.S. and Krishan, G. (1984), Regional Disparities in Level of Socio-economic Development, Vishal Publication, Kurukshetra.

Harvey, H.E. and S.N. Bhardwaj (1973,) Spatial Dimensions of Modernization in a Rural Environment Rajasthan in India', Tijdschrift Voor Economische on Social Geographic, 64, pp. 145-59.

Hoselitz, B.F. (1975), Sociological Aspects of Economic Growth Amerind, New Delhi.

International Labour Office (1977), Meeting Basic Needs: Strategies for Eradications Mass Poverty and Unemployment, ILO, Geneva.

Jayagopal, R. (1990), Human Resources Development: Conceptual Analysis and Strategies. Sterling Publishers, New Delhi.

Krishan, G. (1984) 'Regional disparities in India's in Rice, M.J. (ed.) Geographical Perspective on Development in India, Department of Social Science Education. Thor University of Georgia, pp. 15- 37.

Mazumdar A. and Wasan R. K., Rural Health Services: An Effort Toward Achievement of Health for All by 2000 A.D., Ministry of Health and Family Welfare, New Delhi.

Mishra, G.P. (1985) (ed): Regional Structure of Development and Growth in India, Vol. I and II, Ashish Publishing House, New Delhi.

Mishra, R.P. et al (1974), Regional Development Planning in India: A New Strategy, Vikas, Delhi.

National, Sample Survey (1977), Twenty Fifth Round: July 1970-June

1971, No, 237, National Sample Survey Organization, Department of Statistics, Ministry of Planning, New Delhi.

Notestein, F.W. (1945), 'Population : The Long View' in Shultz. T.W. (ed.) Food for The World, University Press, Chicago.

Planning Commission (1984), Report of the Working Group on District Planning, Government of India, New Delhi.

Presat, R. (1969), Demographic Analysis. Aldine Atherton, Chicago.

Rao, M.V.S. (1977), Socio-Economic Indicators for Development Planning' in National Seminar on Social Statistics, Allied Publishers, Bombay, pp. 183-84.

Raza, M. (1978), Levels of Regional Development in India; paper presented at Indo-Soviet Symposium on Regional Development and National Planning, Tiblis, Baku.

Schwartzberg, J.E. (1962), Three Approaches to the Mapping of Economic Development in Inda, Annals of the Association of American Geographers, 52, pp. 455-68.

Seer, D. (1969), 'The meaning of development' Paper presented at the 11th World Conference of the Society for International Development New Delhi, Nov. 14-17

Singh, L.R. and K.N. Dubey (1985), Demographic Development in a Developing Economy: A Case Study of Uttar Pradesh Population Geography, 7, 27-39.

Social Statistics Division (1977), Data Requirements of the Proposed U.N. System of Social and Demographic Statistics, in National Seminar on Social Statistics, 1, Allied Publishers, Bombay, pp. 82-118.

Thompson, W.S. (1929), 'Population', American Journal of Society, 34. 959-75.

7

Roaming Around the Poverty

ASHOK KUMAR

Since the colonial period, we find that poverty has been our continuing preoccupation. During the national movement, our entire critique and indictment of the colonial system was based on the premise that 'India is a very rich country but its people are very poor'. This was the question or the paradox posed by the early nationalists-by Dadabhai Naoroji, Ranade, Gandhiji, and Nehruji.

Even before Independence, the National Planning Committee, way back in 1938, listed programmes and their targets that would attack poverty as:

— Adequate food consumption for every individual to be raised to not less than 2,400 calories.
— Clothing consumption to be increased from 15 to 30 yards per persons.
— Providing not less than 100 squares feet of housing per individuals, with water supply and sanitation.
— Making education compulsory up to the age of 14.
— Providing, postal communication, insurance, banking and medical facilities.

We may overlook these grandiose scheme as the National Planning Committee has not come to grips with the realities of the situation till then (Prabhakar, 1985).

However, now a days the poverty eradication has become a national slogan and today when we go to the village, we find that people do not believe any more that poverty is god given. They believe that it is man-made. Today the poor tell you, 'we are poor because some others are rich at our expense. Our poverty is the other side of their becoming rich'. This is what we call the explosion of mass consciousness which denotes a sharpening of awareness of growing inequality and the recognition of inegitimate character of inequality. As a result the rich today are different from what they were in the past. The poor are also qualitatively different from what they were in the past.

With this background, we made a distinction between two kinds of poverty: the first is 'natural' poverty which is rooted in a low level of development of our economy, in tremendous unde-development of land, labour and other resources, in tremendous under-utilization of science and technology. This natural poverty can be eradicated only through a developmental programme. The second type of poverty is a 'system generated poverty' which we call 'artificial' poverty. This was a phrase used by Karl Marx. This poverty is there not because the general level of development of economy is low but because the system is such that it makes some people rich and others poor (Joshi, 1985).

Rudolfo Stavenhagen a renowned Mexican sociologist observed that in order to realize what the system produces it is necessary to understand how the system works. 'And this requires giving attention to the other pole of the relationship and perhaps the most important pole; that of the dominant groups'. We shall study those in India who are not poor to understand why so many Indians are poor and must remain so far a long time more. Look at the total system, look at those who have the system in their close, and then look at the poor. But this is what Indian social scientists have not done. They have studied poverty from the outside. They have fashioned measurement scales like; income, calories, assists etc. They have conducted sample surveys and come up with frightening statistical abstractions which apparently have not cost any one a single night's sleep. There is now a host of literature on the Indian poor or rather on Indian poverty, which are not always the same thing. These literatures have helped social scientists to great extent but it has done very little to remove poverty. Nevertheless, poverty studies have helped in the formulation of some of the most acute problems, which is often more urgent than their solution.

In India, the top 10 per cent of the population seems to have the best of all words. Who are these 10 per cent? According to a crude estimates the rural and the urban bourgeoisie constitute some 1.5 per cent of the population. Next in the rank is the so called middle class, which is an amorphous structure. According to Sau (a Mexican economist) 'the Orisie make the upper 10 per cent of the population. Sau's 10 per cent seems to be an understatement. A recent study by the CSO quoted by

Prof. Raj Krishna in an article in 'The Times of India' shows that the group, who lost heavily are the agricultural workers.

As India's rural poor emerge as a proletariat rather than a primarily peasant class, the entire politics of poverty undergoes a tremendous change, and the first big step is taken to make the rural poor less poor. The rural proletariat's struggle will not be for land alone, but for better wages, for employment, for lower prices, against caste and sexual oppression.

The very poor is not India's most acute problem. Whether 52 per cent or 48 per cent or 38 per cent of the Indian population lives in the 1980s below 'poverty line' is not the question but the basic weakness is our planning. It is only allocational and not implementational. We have numerous anti-poverty programmes allocating money. But the structure is behaving more and more in an anti-poverty direction. The new programmes have thrown up parasitic middlemen or intermediaries every where. Many a time there is a tremendous information gap. What you decide at the top is not known to the below. It is one thing to formulate programmes from the top but it is quite another thing to ensure that the programmes you have formulated at the top will operate in the manner in which you desire at the district level, at the block level, at the village level and the household level because your agencies of implementation are either corrupt or weak or do not exist at all.

The two national issues namely security and integrity and removal of poverty are incapably interlinked. In the absence of high priority to internal development in the country, not to be confused with growth rate and per capita income, the inner core of the country which really means a sizable percentage of population, if not the majority will remain weak and for them the issues of their survival and reasonably dignified existence will remain the priority in their own packing order rather than concern for national security and integrity. It is therefore mentioned that unless the two sets of issues are integrated in a determined manner we shall continue to nurse a split picture of India.

To take a critical look at various Poverty Alleviation Programmes and Projects which are directly linked with income and asset generation, employment creation opportunities and there are others which are indirectly linked with the same issue through health care, family welfare, illiteracy removal programmes etc. Numerous evaluation studies carried out by official and un-official agencies measure the effectiveness of these programmes in terms of physical and financial targets. These studies hard ever critically examine the structure and the process of functioning (efficiency criterion) of the delivery system which at the apex are the Ministries in the centre and Departments in the state and at the bottom level the functionaries operating at the grass-root level. A major if not the most vital, component in incrementally reducing the poverty in rural and urban areas will be to pay attention to administrative system, and develop some sensible, practical and acceptable innovative measures.

One may either take up the issue in the form of revising the definition of poverty line, another person may try to rationalize it by maintaining that such observations are not unexpected in a vast country like India and a third person may like to pay attention to these incompetent and irresponsible officials. We shall devote ourselves to the third approach attention to the delivery system and provide alternative formulations regarding certain aspects of the delivery system.

Among the multiple agencies these schemes are similar and there are others which are not so. The overall target population below the poverty line being the same. These multiple agencies approach them casually or otherwise with their plans or packages of plans without any reference to what other schemes from other departments are responded to, by the same target group. To sum up we operate the complex key board of a piano with all the reads playing at the same time producing different sounds resulting in high noise level (for official records and mass media) and not an orchestrated piece of music. There are many flag-ships roaming around on the ocean of poverty if that is the picture in a state it is equally so in the centre. It is therefore, suggested that the key to the success of anti-poverty strategy and programmes lies in creating not only relevant programmes reflecting the interest of the masses but also to create the new types of human resource development for the Programme Implementation.

8

Removal of Rural Unemployment through Jawahar Rozgar Yojana

MUKTA MITTAL & ASHOK KUMAR

Since the inception of the planning provision of employment generation has engaged the attention of planners and policy-makers. The Sixth Plan (1980-85) gave a new impetus and direction to the employment generation efforts and introduced, for the first time, the NREP and the RLEGP programmes on a countrywide basis. The Seventh Plan envisaged providing employment to all the unemployed in the rural areas. About 45 per cent of the employment generation was expected from the investments in the agricultural sector and the rest from the specific programmes of NREP and RLEGP. The outlays during the first three years of the Seventh Plan for both the programmes have been stepped up and were around Rs. 1,200 crores per annum which generated about 600 million man days of employment each year. The target of employment generation from the agricultural sector, however, would fall short of the expectations particularly because of insufficient allocations.

The Jawahar Rozgar Yojana (JRY) has come at a time when the goverment is pressing ahead for the establishment of the Panchayat Raj System. This scheme has ostensibly been started to commemorate the birth anniversary of our first Prime Minister. Besides, when the Government talks of the upliftment of the very poor, especially in the rural areas, it indicates that an election year is round the corner. However, the feature of the Jawaher Rozgar Yojana (JRY) unfolded by the Prime Minister, in Parliament recently reflect the government's anxiety to give a push to the effort at generating rural employment.

The Programme

What exactly is the Jawahar Rozgar Yojana? This is an employment programme announced in the Budget. The idea is to reach out to the poorest sections of society by providing employment for at least one person every family for at least 50 days. The Centre's contribution will be Rs. 2,100 crores, about 80 per cent the total outlay of Rs. 2,625 crores. The states are to contribute the rest. The funds are to be provided directly to the village panchayats and a village with an average population of 3,000 to 4,000 will receive anything between Rs. 80, 000 and Rs. 1,00,000 per year. Funds are to be developed to states on the basis of the level of poverty and backwardness of the people. In spatial coverage, it to be put into operation throughout the country. Its benefits will reach "every single panchayat". As estimated 440 lakh families are expected to benefit from the scheme. This scheme is going to be a comprehensive decentralized one for rural employment, and the existing two main employment programmes i.e. National Rural Employment Programme (NREP), and the Rural Landless Employment Guarantee Programme (RLEGP) are to be merged with the Jawahar Rozgar Yojana.

Thus, the Jawahar Rozgar Yojana is a combination of all employment programmes, especially NREP and RLEGP. This clubbing can be justified if these two programmes are unqualified failures and if this scheme adds substantially to the outlay. NREP has been acclaimed by our Plan documents as a success in terms of fulfilment of targets. Further nearly Rs. 1,600 crores had been marked in 1987-88 for these schemes already, which means that the addition of the remaining Rs. 1,025 crores would be the only new element. Instead, the same amount could have been distributed to the existing schemes.

However, while a lot of rhetoric has gone into propagating this move at all levels , a succinct evaluation is required. The scheme is to be looked at from the following angles: Whether this scheme has anything new to offer whether the mathematics of the scheme is convincing; whether people will really gain from this move; and whether it is economically speaking, a rational step. It is in this view, the present exercise has undertaken.

Characteristic of the Jawahar Rozgar Yojana

The Prime Minister has admitted that the level of leakages have been extremely high in our welfare programmes. He has put the figure as high as 80 per cent. While this may be an exaggeration, a 30-40 per cent level may be a more accurate figure. But merely remaining a programme one can not do away with leakages. The logical think to do

in this context is to plug the loopholes in the existing system and prevent delays by timely disbursements. However, the main characteristic of the Jawahar Rozgar Yojana are as follows:

(i) **The scheme aims at placing in the hands of village panchayats throughout the country and adequate funds to be provided to run their own rural employment schemes. Every panchayat with a population of 3,000 to 4,000 would receive between Rs. 80,000 to Rs. 1,00,000 per year.**

(ii) **The total central assistance for the scheme is Rs. 2,100 crores for the financial year 1989-90.**

(iii) Devaluation of funds to the states in the Yojana will be determined in proportion to the size of the population below the poverty line, the proportion of scheduled castes, tribes and agricultural labourers and the level of agricultural productivity. Also, the Yojana envisages to provide special consideration to the requirements of hills, deserts and Islands.

(iv) The scheme proposes to benefit those members of the rural households who presently get employment for less than six months in a year. One member of such households will be provided employment for 50 to 100 days in a year.

(v) A little less than one third or 30 per cent of employment generated to be reserved for women.

The decentralised nature of the programme is the most important plank on which the Jawahar Rozgar Yojana is formulated. The panchayats will be entrusted with the task of formulating and implementing their need-based schemes of employment generation. With the passing of the bill for bringing about constitutional amendments to the Panchayati Raj System in the recently cancelled Lok Sabha, the panchayats are expected to work more democratically with direct elections for all the seats including those of the scheduled castes, tribes and women, who have also been granted reservation. For the first time, therefore, the under-privileged sections of the rural society will have a common platform of the basis of equality and not as nominated members of the upper echelons. Such an elected body will be provided funds for implementing the schemes.

The Programme Implementation

The central assistance of the Jawahar Rozgar Yojana will finance

80 per cent of the total. This is scin contrast to the existing arrangement. Presently, the NREP is being financed on 50:50 sharing basis between the centre and the states and the RLEGP entirely by the state government. Now, in fact, the state government's role in the Jawahar Rozgar Yojana is only of contributing the 20 per cent share. The panchayat's accountability to the state government is not explicitly detailed out in the Jawahar Rozgar Yojana. The bureaucracy which was completely involved in the formulation of implementation of the NREP and the RLEGP has been left high and dry. Who would provide the technical expertise and guidance for preparing the shelf of projects? Who will take over the role of contractors and intermediaries? What machinery will be set up for redressing the grievances of rural poor under the programme? Those questions remain unanswered. The data base on agricultural productivity and the number of days of employment held by the rural poor are not available with the panchayats.

The fact that the panchayats now will wield a clout over the funds may also in no way make the Rozgar Yojana more effective. The Yojana, as announced, makes no mention of the monitoring of the funds. It goes without saying that a programme of such a magnitude needs close monitoring.

The Economic of the JRY

The economics of the Jawahar Rozgar Yojana is very puzzling. Let us assume that only one person from a family is provided employment. There would hence be 440 lakh workers. At a conservative level, let us further assume that no one gets more than, say, 50 days of employment. This comes to 22,000 workdays. The wage rate is to vary from Rs. 9.80 to Rs. 27.50 depending on the location of the scheme. Assuming the wage rate to be Rs. 9.80, the total cost of the scheme at the base minimum would be Rs. 2,156 crores, affording a leverage of about Rs. 470 crores for expenditure on materials. The Seventh Plan document had stated that nearly 50 per cent of the expenditure was usually used up on materials, which has also been assumed in this project. That way it should be about Rs. 1.310 crores. But, going by the minimum standards laid down by Rozgar Yojana, this would not be possible since only Rs. 470 crores would be available for materials. Can we economize to this extent.

Alternatively, let us assume that we meet the basic norm laid down by the planners viz. that at least 50 per cent of the cost is on material. Then there will be two options: we can fix the employment levels at 22,000 mandays and the wage level can be determined by the amount which can be spent i.e. Rs. 1,312 crores. Then the wage level works out to be Rs. 5.96 per head per day, which works out to about Rs. 180 a month. Even if we irrationally assume an average family of four in the rural areas, the family would still be stuck below the poverty line; alternatively, we can assume the norm of Rs. 9.80 as the wage rate to ensure that the person receiving it will remain above the poverty line, provided that the family size is four. In this case, only about 270 lakh workers can be employed, which again goes against what has been proposed. What can be seen from the arithmetic is that the scheme cannot satisfy all objectives. In the calculations we have made very simplifying assumptions, viz. there are no leakages in the form of dishonesty; and the selection process is impeccable in all respects. This is certainly not true because all over employment programmes like NREP, RLEGP and IRDP have been played by adverse selection procedures. Further, there is no inbuilt mechanism to ensure that the same family gets selected in each of the years. If one has to be gainfully employed to remain above the poverty line, most of the assumptions made above have to be adjusted. In fact, this scheme of providing work for 50 days a year will work in the restricted way, provided the same family can get employment in the remaining part of the year. Thus JRY will run into the problem of keeping a family above the poverty line in a given year even when the norms are met because 50 days income cannot keep a family even at the subsistence level. At least, it could plug up the days during which the workers are seasonally unemployed. If this is the aim of the scheme, then it has not been stated clearly as it holds out promises of a different nature.

Since the wage spread will average between Rs. 9.80 and Rs. 27.50 further complications are bound to arise in any case. To look at the economics of the programme, let us assume that all the 440 lakh families get employment at the rate of Rs. 9.80 a day are pulled above the poverty line. This would mean that the material cost would be closed to nothing. This strategy tentamounts to the Keynesian prescription of digging up holes, only to fill them up. There will be no corresponding increase onto the supply side. Even useful construction activities like building of schools, community center etc. will be stalled since there will not be any funds left once other objectives are satisfied. If this is the case it would closely resemble an unemployment dole. At a general level we would only be adding to the demand pressure, which would have an adverse effect on the price level, however small it may be. This is because when Keynes proposed such idle schemes, it was at a time when there was a worldwide depression and shortage of aggregate demand. In this case there is no such problem and there appears to no economic rationale behind such a scheme. In fact, there will be a good incentive for the poor to remain poor to qualify for the scheme.

Critical Evaluation

In formulating the programme, the Union Government has completely sidetracked the Planning Commission. It has ignored the finance ministry and most importantly, it has bypassed the state governments too. Further, the government has cleverly jettisoned two existing employment generation programmes, marginally increased budgetary allocation of this score and come up with a revolutionary scheme providing massive employment to the poor in rural India. In essence the JRY is nothing but old wine in a new bottle. But in order to send out an unambiguous signal to the rural areas that the funds are flowing from Delhi, the Union government has decided to leapfrog state governments and release the funds directly to the Panchayats.

On the face of if the new employment generation programme to be implemented by panchayats is quite an improvement over the earlier approaches. But how will it all function. On one has to wait and see when the new panchayats are elected and start implementing this and other programmes. It is quite well-known that panchayat as a unit of local self-government was introduced after independence to give village folks some measures of role in taking decision relating to their daily lives. However, over the years this institution has been allowed to grow for various reasons, political and non political. Except for some of the north-eastern states the institution of panchayat has been introduced by almost all the states and Union Territories. However, for the past 10-12 years elections have not been held for these, and hence with a few exceptions most of the panchayats are relatively non-functional.

Under the new programme, not only do the funds flow directly from the centre, to the DRDAs but the criterion for allocation of funds to the 440 districts in the country stands modified. The allocation is now directly linked to the incidence of poverty determined on a new proxy index of backwardness devised by the Department of Rural Development. It is this new criterion for allocation of funds that has come under severe criticism from opposition — rule states. According to Kerala four rural employment schemes would be considerably reduced. As against the earlier allotment of Rs. 60.50 crore under the twin employment schemes, the state gets only Rs. 50.48 crore. But Kerala has the largest number of unemployed in the country and in therefore entitled to more central assistance. Alleging that the centre has adopted a discriminatory attitude in releasing funds for the new pre-programme, Mr. Nayanar said while the share of Andhra Pradesh and Tamil Nadu has gone down by over 2 per cent and 1 per cent respectively that of Utter Pradesh and Madhya Pradesh has gone up by over 2 per cent and 15 per cent respectively. Even in the case of West Bengal, it was proposed that the total allocation of funds would be Rs. 2,100 crore but according to the latest decision, that total allocation funds would be Rs. 1,600 crore only.

The indicators of poverty adopted by the centre to decide on the allocation of funds may not be all that accurate and can be quite misleading at the village level. For example, the programme uses the proportion of scheduled castes and scheduled tribes to total population as a measure of backwardness. Even though they do constitute to poorest sections of our rural society, their condition may not be uniform in every village. The population of depressed classes, agricultural workers, agricultural productivity per hectar are some of the yardsticks being used for measuring the poverty level. Already reports from Maharashtra say that the highly backward and neglected districts of Ratnagiri and Sindhudurg have been classified as the least backward of all districts in the state under the programme. More such complaints are likely to emerge. But going by the drum beating that is currently on vis a vis the JRY, such complaints are not likely to force the centre to change the determining the backwardness of a region.

Another important aspect of this scheme is to check the migration of rural labour to metropolitan cities which are already choking with heavy population pressure. Again one will have to wait and see how far this scheme is able to check the migration of rural labour and to what extent.

Concluding Remarks

The Scenario which emerges from the above discussions that the government has finally got hold of the margin ball and by placing power and funds in the hands of panchayats, the panacea for all the ills of employment generation programmes has been found. We, however, know from our past experience, that decentralization at the village level has not succeeded so far. The cosmetic changes which have been brought out may have little positive impact unless the issues plaguing the Panchayat Raj institutions as well as the existing employment generation programmes are also dealt with. The leadership of the panchayats has always seen in the hands of more affluent sections of the rural society and these leaders have willingly perpetuated the incautious socio-economic structure in the rural areas. The responsibility of running the Yojana will only to strengthen their hands. It is also too far-fetched to expect that once the SCs and STs will be elected to the panchayats, they will have the power or an equal say in the decision-making process. The fact of the matter is that even now these under-privileged sections of the rural society are economically dependent upon the better off socio economy groups. They invariably indebted to them. The scheduled caste families get employment either in their land or through them in other places. Their female members also work as labourers and some even work as servants.

However, in brief, the above arguments indicate that JRY basically has nothing new to offer. It is simply a case of merging paretically successful schemes into one and rechristening it to rake up the pop nationalism. Its economics is highly dubious. The programmes has all rural into the problem of not being able to satisfy the objective of employment generation in terms of the number of workers employed owing to the constraints of minimum wages, total funds at its disposal, minimum number of days for which employment has to be provided and fixed cost of materials. But will the man on the street understand this? Thus, we concentrate our efforts on propagating a scheme which lacks the basic prerequisites for success.

References

1. K.V. Rao, (1989): JRY-Old Wine in New Bottle, Business Standard, June 11, 1989, p. 5.

2. Sabnavis Madan (1989), 'Rozgar Yojana: The Real Motives, Financial Express, June 13, 1989.
3. *Ibid.*, p. 5.
4. J.S. Sodhi (1989), 'Jawahar Rozgar Yojana: Panacea for Rural Unemployment 's, Economic Times, June 10,1989.
5. Sabnavis, op. cit.
6. Rao, op., cit.
7. See, Business Standard, June 1,1989.

9

Is IRDP a Better Alternative for Rural Development?

PURNA C. PRADHAN &RAJENDRA P. MAMGAIN

I

According to Planning Commission estimates, 48 per cent of the people in rural areas and 41 per cent in urban areas in this country live below the poverty line. The magnitude of poverty is further evident from the census reported that more than four-fifths of our population are living in rural areas, spread over six lakh villages. In rural areas about nine-tenths of the population depend on agriculture for their livelihood.

Apart from the fact that the majority of the agricultural holdings in the country are small and marginal (less than two hectares), an estimated 100 million hectares of the land fall in the arid or semi-arid zone, and another 25 million hectares are food-prone, it is equally noteworthy that 70 per cent of the country's gross cultivated area is entirely dependent on unpredictable rainfall with no means of irrigation.

When we talk about the rural poor, therefore, the reference is to small and marginal farmers with their uneconomic holdings tenants, share-croppers, landless agricultural labourers and rural artisans. Among them are a substantial number of persons belonging to scheduled castes and scheduled tribes, as also the rural working women, subject to exploiting for ages.

To make a dent on rural poverty, however, number of programmes were tried out in the past. There are the Community Development Programmes, the Intensive Agriculture Development Programme, the Small Farmers Development Agency, the Marginal Farmers Development Agency, the Drought-Prone Areas Programme, and the Command Area Development Programme. While they did bring some benefits to certain sections of the population, by and large, they failed to make the desired impact. It is after years of trials with a series of programmes, the

IRDP has been conceived as one of the best means of reaching the vast masses of the people.

The present paper is based on an empirical study undertaken by the authors and attempts to discuss the failure of one of the programmes i.e. SFDA in Sambalpur district of Orissa and the remedial steps taken by the Government to overcome some of the problem. The data presented in this paper relating to SFDA are up to the year 1981-82 i.e. till the merger of this agency with the DRDA.

II

Agricultural development holds the key to economic prosperity of the people of Orissa as 80 per cent of the population depends on it for their livelihood. Quite clearly a system's approach to agricultural development involving physical factors, social engineering, skills, knowledge and change agent is imperative. Optimum combination of these factors would ensure rapid strides in agriculture. Mere Green Revolution, however, is not adequate if the goal of socio-economic justice is to be achieved. The social imbalances within the agricultural community have to be set right. It is in this context that the role of small and marginal farmers assumes importance. The Small Farmers Development Agency is a conscious attempt to direct developmental efforts towards small and marginal farmers.

SFDA started operating in Sambalpur district, from January 1975. In the district, nearly 65 per cent of households derive their income from agriculture. More than 87 per cent of the agriculturists own within 10 acres of land, comprising 52 per cent of the total agricultural land. This means that, a few own almost half of the agricultural land with bulk of the population sharing the other half. Hardly one-fifth of the net sown area is irrigated. Out of the 29 blocks of the district, only 11 are served by the Hirakud Canal system with an average of 1,09,—288 hectares. The other blocks are rainfed.

Credit requirement for cultivation is mostly met by the banks. curiously most of these banks are situated in urban area. For instance, out of 38 branches of Commercial Banks, 21 are located inside Sambalpur town. So a majority of small and marginal farmers have been left out of the purview of formal credit institutions.

SFDA has been working in the district since 1975 in the above background. The purpose of the agency is to help small and marginal farmers, agricultural labourers, and rural artisans improve their living standards. This has been done under different schemes covering agriculture, animal husbandry and rural industries. Eligible members are being identified and given help under different schemes by various district institutions. Broadly speaking most of the schemes are credit oriented.

The area of operation of SFDA in the beginning was confined to 16 non-irrigated blocks (out of a total of 29 blocks). It had covered 159 gram panchayats in 2,061 villages with a population of 8.08 lakhs. During 1980-81 all the 29 blocks of the district were covered.

The performance of SFDA shows the following trend: upto the end of 1981, 44,952 small farmers, 52,490 marginal farmers, 3,021 agricultural labourers, 23 non-agricultural labourers, 32 rural artisans and 955 others had been enrolled as members of cooperative societies. During 1980-81 the total credit mobilized under the programme was Rs. 167.25 lakhs. The share of the cooperative banks was Rs. 92.24 lakhs and that of regional rural and commercial banks was Rs. 75.01 lakhs.

The number of farmers motivated to adopt HYV, as at the end of the year 1981, stood at 14,559 small farmers, and 7,954 marginal farmers. During the same period SFDA has also adopted crop demonstration as an important teaching aid in introducing high-yielding and improved varieties of crops in the fields of 1826 farmers. Input subsidy was also provided by the SFDA to supply improved HYV seeds, fertilizers, pesticides and implements to small and marginal farmers at a reduced rate. SFDA made available 3,779 sets of different agricultural implements, 1,137 pairs of bullocks, 146 bullock carts, 12,421 dug wells, 421 pump sets, and 33 lift irrigation projects during the same period to the farmers.

Though more than two lakh members had been identified in the district, only half had enrolled themselves as members of the cooperatives. The wide gap between the number of people identified and those enrolled needs to be explained here, connected with this main issue are three sub-issues. In that the people are reluctant to become members? And if so, what are the factors which inhibit them? Or, is it that they are not properly educated about the need and importance of becoming members of these change agents? And if so, why do these change agents behave in a manner contrary to what is expected of them? Or, is it due to the ineffective and unhelpful attitudes of the cooperative societies towards these small farmers. It is rather difficult to explain the gaps exclusively in terms of any one of these reasons. It is generally a combination of all these variables that would lead to the gaps. In the SFDA scheme, more than 60 per cent of the total expenditure had been spent on minor irrigation. However, only half the number of dug wells financed had been completed. Similarly, many community irrigation projects and dug wells had been a continuing feature since the inception of the agency.

In the case of improved implements, their adoption depends not only on the knowledge of their advantages which is easy to acquire also on the availability of these articles and the capacity of the people to pay for them. SFDA had only supplied 3,779 sets of different improved agricultural implements, whereas 96,125 farmers were identified as eligible for the benefit. Further, efforts to popularize different types or agricultural implements has not been enough to meet the magnitude of the needs. Defective loaning system, lack of purchasing capacity, non-availability of improved implement and fragmentation of holdings are the four main causes of inadequate usage of the improved implements by farmers.

Cooperative societies are the premier institutions through which a major part of the credit is distributed. Evidently, however, the cooperatives in the dry areas are either dormant or non-viable cooperative societies are not providing maximum benefit to small and marginal farmers.

In the course of our discussion with a number of farmer, two important issues came to light. These are the class and caste structure of the rural society in relation to cooperative endeavours. In the agricultural sector, three broad classes emerge, the big landed, the small landed and the landless. The big landed class has the necessary economic clout to secure a high status for itself and occupy a commanding position in all spheres of activity. The landless class. The small landed class must also do so if it is to survive.

Caste also determines in some way the structure and function of rural cooperative societies. Of the several caste groups, the higher castes have greater representation in the management committee of the society. As regards assistance to farmers, cooperative societies operate against members of the lower castes. The dominant class and caste groups were opposed to the very concept of uplift of the weaker sections. The National Commission of Agriculture had identified the sociological constrants to the smooth functiong of co-operatives in the country. It observed that the present structure was not oriented to meeting the needs of weaker section.

The behaviour of banks is also equally important in helping the small farmers since banks have to finance the schemes formulated by SFDA. Though banks have been directed to extend all possible assistance, it was observed that the approach of banks was not uniforms in all the places. What was more surprising branches of the same bank pursued different policies in different places. Officials were asked to explain why the farmers were not able to take advantage of the banking facilities. The following reasons were given:

> Non-availability of "patta", ineffective functioning of cooperative societies, non-availability of surety and security, bureaucratic red tape and reluctance on the part of farmers to take advantage of loan facilities.
>
> The system of communication is also ineffective in the district. Radio, newspaper and pamphlets had only a limited influence on small farmers. A majority of them had no radios in their houses. The low degree of literacy meant that they could not learn anything through newspapers and published literature.
>
> Some of the small farmers, who were ignorant of the schemes and procedures, were asked why those who were aware of the schemes and procedures did not divulge the information to them. Their reply was that there was none who had the village interest in his heart. Everyone was interested in himself and his kinsmen.
>
> Marketing arrangements for products are very poor. Though this affects every section of the poor farming community. Small farmers are affected in greater measure. They sell the produce at a lower price immediately after harvest, buy for consumption at a later date at higher prices, and sometimes hypothecate their crops against credit taken earlier. Those cultivators who denied an access to the formal credit market rely heavily on local credit markets and inevitably get lower prices for their products.

III

Despite all its shortcoming, SFDA might have still helped in the upliftment of small farmers, but obviously its impact on rural disparities has been marginal. It was, therefore, felt that a programme to provide assistance to the rural poor irrespective of whether they were farmers or artisans or craftsmen was required and the integrated rural development programme was seen as a response to this need.

IRDP is aimed at the poorest among the poor, mainly scheduled castes and scheduled tribes, agricultural labourers, small farmers, marginal farmers, rural artisans and craftsmen. The programme, initially taken up on 2,300 blocks in the country in areas covered by special programmes like SFDA, DPAP and CAD, was extended to all the 5.011 development blocks on the Gandhi Jayanti in 1980.

10

Can IRDP Becomes More Relevant?

DR. K.M. GEORGE

Growth with social justice has been the basic plan objective in India. In fact, reduction in the incidence of poverty and its ultimate elimination is the national goal. Planning Commission has arrived at the norm that family having annual income of Rs. 6,400 or less (at 1984-85 prices) is to be considered as one below the poverty line. Using the households consumption expenditure data collected by NSS in its 38th round (1983). On the basis of the 32nd and 39th Rounds of National Sample Survey, the percentage of rural population below the poverty line has declined from 51.2 in 1977 to 40.4 in 1983-84. The Seventh Five Year Plan started with 222.2 million persons below the poverty line who constituted 39.9% of the rural population. The Plan projects that by 1990-91, the percentage of population below the poverty line in the rural areas will come down to 28.5% and the long-term objective is that by 1994-95, it would be further brought down to 10% and hopefully it will be completely eliminated by 2000 AD.

IRDP was first introduced in 1978-79 in a few selected districts and was later extended throughout the country by 1980-81. In the seven years ending 1986-87, nearly 25 million families have been given self-employment assistance under IRDP involving a total investment of Rs. 8,218 crores of which the bank credit alone amounts to Rs. 5,240 crores. Last year, the credit mobilisation under the programme was of the order of Rs. 1,000 crores. Such a major intervention by the government in favour of the poor is probably unparalleled anywher-else in the world. The implementation of the programme has shown that it has been fulfilling the targets both in physical and financial terms.

Our Planners have always avoided the hard options of a radical nature and opted for soft solutions. They have, for example, avoided radical land reforms and structural changes and opted for special programmes for the poor, and also opted for isolated anti-poverty programmes instead of introducing rigorous and highly systematical and comprehensive planning at various levels. In short, they have chosen a developmental process which is of least resistance and which favours the vested interests of the power elite. The complexities of the present problems, however, suggest that we cannot go on like this for ever. The time has now arrived when we have to make hard choices for our developmental path. The policies which just scratch the system on the surface will no more deliver the goods. We have to not accept that unless we change our path towards the interest of the masses of the poor, we will not be able to face the challenge of poverty eradication. Unless we put a brake to the indiscriminate high-tech growth process, and choose a path that provides ample employment opportunities for the poor, we will not be able to eradicate poverty of the masses'.

This is the background of gauging the height of IRDP. Under this the efficiency of investment and recasting of IRDP are also examined. However, one should critically evaluate the impact of the direct intervention programmes meant for poverty alleviation before coming to policy recommendations of reshaping IRDP.

The thrust under IRDP is to bring about qualitative improvement in the implementation of the programme by strengthening the backward and forward linkages, diversifying activities under the programme by emphasising on the secondary and tertiary sectors. National level committees have been set up for animal husbandry, horticulture and small scale industries to forge stronger linkages between the infrastructural facilities available and the beneficiaries under these sectors in different parts of the country. Intensive work of introducing sericulture in areas where it is feasible to promote it has been undertaken so as to bring this as one of the major activities for the IRDP beneficiaries.

During the year 1987-88 special efforts were made to monitor the assistance given to the very poor. Supplementary dose of credit was given to families assisted during the Sixth Five Year Plan period but continued to be below the poverty line for not fault of theirs. The limit for security free loans under IRDP has been raised from Rs. 5,000 to 10,000 for agriculture and allied activities. The scheme for strengthening the block machinery and Monitoring Cell at the State Headquarters also continued. The target for 1987-88 was to assist 39 lacs of families comprising over 29 lacs old beneficiaries of the Sixth Plan and 9.96 lakh new beneficiaries. An allocation of Rs. 310.60 crores has been provided in the central sector. The total allocation including the state share for the implementation of the IRDP was Rs. 613.38 crores. Term credit of the order of Rs. 981.82 crores was expected to be mobilised for the implementation of the programme during the year 1987-88. The achievements under IRDP are presented in Table 1.

Table 1

Targets and Achievements of IRDP in 1987–88
Rs. in Crores

	Details	*Annual target*	*Achievement till Jan. '88*	*% age*
A.	Financial progress allocations (Central & States)	613.38	477.68	77.88
	Release of Central Share	310.60	269.54	86.77
	Credit	981.82	783.28	79.81
B.	Physical progress families to be assisted (Nos. in lakhs)	39.11	29.02	74.22
	a) Coverage of SC\STs to the total assisted	30%	12.46	42.92
	b) Coverage of Women families to the total assisted	30%	4.82	16.61

Source: Annual Report, Govt. of India, Department of Rural Development, 1987-88, p. 17.

The percentage of families assisted was 74.22. Against a target of 30% coverage for SC/STs to the total assisted, the achievement was 42.92%. However, coverage of women families to the total assisted was 16.61% only.

Details of physical and financial progress under IRDP during 1987-88 till January' 88 are presented in appendix-1-3. The data are given State and Union Territory wise. The various parameters presented, include central and state shares, utilisation, total families assisted, coverage of SC/ST and women as well as disbursement of term credit by co-operatives and commercial banks.

Improvements in Programme Implementation

With a view to improving the implementation of IRDP, the Department of Rural Development, Ministry of Agriculture has taken up a monthly concurrent evaluation of the programme from October 1985 onwards. It is expected that the concurrent evaluation study will continue for one more year. The second round of concurrent evaluation of IRDP was undertaken from January' 87. The survey was conducted by selected research institutions all over the country. Every month 72 blocks from 36 districts on a rotating and random a basis are selected. A sample of 40 beneficiaries from two blocks in a district, i.e. 20 old beneficiaries and 20 new beneficiaries are selected on random basis for the collection of data. Six monthly concurrent evaluation of IRDP for January-June, 1987 was prepared covering a sample of 8, 086 beneficiaries. based on the study findings, the following steps were taken to improve the implementation.

- — The uniform application cum approval form for IRDP borrowers has been introduced with effect from 1st April, 1987.
- — The limit for security free loan has been raised from Rs. 5,000 to Rs. 10,000 for agricultural and allied activities.
- — A format of Master Policy cum agreement for livestock assets has been finalised and circulated to all State Governments for adoption.
- — To facilitate proper disbursement of the assets, the banks have fixed one day in a week for disbursement purpose under IRDP though the processing of applications and sanction of loans will continue throughout the month.
- — In order to expedite the pace of communication to and from the DRDAs telex facility is being introduced.
- — The mini computer centres would be set up in DRDAs using funds available under administrative infrastructure. Computerisation of the basic data of Rural Development Schemes at the district level will make it possible to monitor the progress and quality of these programmes.
- — Diversification of activities to include new and innovative programmes like fruit processing units, fish farming etc. would be encouraged.
- — Close dialogue and coordination between DRDA and the employment exchange for employment opportunities and training under TRYSEM will be initiated.
- — Setting up special teams/missions for formulation of major projects on pilot basis for a few selected districts will be started on a priority

basis.

— Stipend/honorarium payable under TRYSEM has been enhanced in 1987.

— A computer model for block level planning has been prepared and circulated to the States. Project Directors have been exposed to this model.

— The beneficiary has also opt for continuance of insurance for animals even after he has paid off the loan, at concessional rates of premium, for a further period of three years after the closure of the loan account.

Institutional Finance for IRDP

Financial assistance under IRDP is provided by the banking institutions. They include Commercial Banks, Co-operatives and Regional rural banks. Credit mobilisation till December 1987 was nearly Rs. 690 crores against the target of Rs. 982 crores. This is likely to increase substantially based on the achievement of Rs. 1,014 crores over a target of Rs. 870 crores in 1986-87. With a view to removing the constraints and streamlining the procedures close liaison is maintained with the Finance Ministry, Reserve Bank of India and NABARD. The credit linkages has been made compulsory in North Eastern Region with effect from April 1985. It has been decided with the approval of RBI to permit DRDAs to perform loaning functions on behalf of banks in unbanked blocks in Arunachal Pradesh, Nagaland and Manipur. Thus DRDAs will draw and disburse money to IRDP borrowers and recover the loans.

A pilot project for disbursement of loan and subsidy in cash was introduced on an experimental basis in 22 blocks with effect from 1st April 1986. According to the evaluation study conducted by Reserve Bank of India in January-February 1987 it was observed that cash disbursement has some good features such as elimination of leakages and satisfaction of beneficiary in acquiring asset of his own choice. However, the study also reported some adverse aspects like diversification of cash for consumption purposes. A subsequent study again conducted by the RBI in November 1987 pointed out that the post-disbursement supervision of assets by financing banks, which is an essential feature of the scheme was not effective due to pressure of work on the bank staff. The RBI, therefore, advised against extension of cash disbursement scheme to more blocks.

Simplification of Procedure

Department of Rural Development of the Government of India constituted a committee under the Chairmanship of Secretary, Rural Development to suggest simplification of procedures under IRDP. Senior officials of Banking Division, RBI and some Commercial Banks were the members of the committee.

The working group on Lead Bank Scheme set up by the Banking Division of the Ministry of Finance has submitted a report suggesting certain structural changes in the various coordination committees. Various parameters relating to credit such as bankwise distribution of loan, repayment schedule, level of overdues, insurance of assets and the like were monitored though the concurrent evaluation. It was observed that 81 per cent beneficiaries had found the financial assistance sufficient for acquiring the assets. About 44 per cent families had no overdues, 31 per cent had overdues less than Rs. 1,000. However, one area which continues to cause concern is lower repayment schedules prescribed by the Bank. The concurrent evaluation reveals that the repayment period was less than 3 years in 15 per cent cases, and just three years in 33 per cent cases.

Insurance of Assets

The General Insurance Corporation of India and its four subsidiaries provide insurance cover for the assets under IRDP. So far as livestock assets are concerned, a format of Master Policy has been finalised and circulated to all State Governments. Under the Master Policy, IRDP beneficiaries are entitled to concessional rates of premium. If the beneficiaries have any animal other than the one acquired under IRDP, he can avail concessional rates of premium for these animals also.

Further the beneficiary can continue the insurance cover at concessional rate after the closure of the loan account if the animals do not exceed insurable age limit. The claim procedure has been simplified to secure expeditious disposal of claims.

Intervention Strategies

The Public Accounts Committee (PAC) of Parliament has made some recommendations about the reshaping of IRDP in one of its reports[2]. The PAC observed that the IRDP approach was defective on account of a number of reasons. They include non-comprehensive approach, multiplicity of agencies with poor coordination and the like. The committee further added that, "the programme which does not help poor households cross the poverty line in one-go, cannot carry its credibility as to its validity and hence credibly outlays rural elementary needs of the IRDP". The PAC also highlighted the implementational problems encountered by IRDP like inadequate infrastructural support, poor administration of second dose of assistance, great hurry at the end of the financial year etc. Besides, organisational problems also came in for sharp criticism by the PAC.

People's participation should be encouraged through beneficiary level participation. Infact, the representations of people in local self-government do not necessarily represent the interests of the poor and they tend to go against the interests of the poor to favour the interests of their own class. According to critics the scope for IRDP is limited. Based on the present developmental process, IRDP remains the only instrument in reaching out the poorest of the poor with some measure of success. Genuine voluntary organisations if associated with IRDP can play a very significant role in making the delivery system efficient[3].

Action through voluntary sector is also an important means of channelising public participation in poverty alleviation programmes. Recognising the importance of the voluntary sector, 10% of the funds of Rural Development programmes has been earmarked for this purpose. The funding of voluntary organisations in taking up poverty alleviations programmes is done through CAPART. CAPART has been able to identify and evaluate the capabilities of voluntary organisations in the country and has been continuously interacting with them to increase the level of participation from the voluntary sector in the programme. There is a scope for further increase in the participation by the voluntary organisations in the programme.

The contribution of IRDP to lift the beneficiaries above the poverty line depends on the income levels of the households during the pre-loan period and the scale of financial assistance rendered apart from the efficiency of the performance of the assets financed. Despite the low level of income inadequate access to working capital, a relatively large proportion of IRDP assets under the primary sector which are relatively more risk and leakage prone, are found to be intact with the poorer households. This may be explained by the economic viability of such enterprises for the poor on account of labour intensity and scale neutrality of these activities as well as the familiarity of the poor with the skills needed for running such traditional enterprises[4]. It can be said with confidence that the success of any poverty alleviation programme should be judged by the extent to which, at the end of the plan period, the assets skill distribution pattern becomes more egalitarian and equitable. In the case of IRDP it is necessary to think in terms of assets other than land because its capacity to absorb additional claims is meagre. Besides, greater attention needs to be paid to upgradation of traditional skills and imparting new skills which are required for diversification of rural economy and sustaining its viability. As a matter of policy poverty alleviation should become the major aim of development and not mearly a separable component of the Five Year Plans. In fact, it should become an integral part of a single plan whose major aim would be to create a more egalitarian structure, which would mean not merely removing poverty but removing the causes which generate poverty. Poverty crossing would be a shortlived phenomenon if the causes of poverty are not eliminated and the poor are unable to acquire assets and skills which will help them to earn and live a decent livelihood[5].

On the whole the performance under the Integrated Rural Developmental Programme has been impressive in terms of financial and physical parameters. Nonetheless, the grey areas still continue to contain the effectiveness of the programme.

It is an accepted fact that the direct intervention strategies meant for poverty alleviation has created an impact. As brought out in a number of studies based on the data bearing on several indicators of performance of IRDP, scholars have attempted comprehensive analysis of these results for different states.

Kurian (1987) in his analysis of different states has established beyond doubt the relevance of IRDP, when he observes, "IRDP can not only provide assets to the poor families but also can create awareness among the poor about the possibility of a better life and their right to achieve it and the means of achieving it"[6]. The fact therefore, remains that IRDP has really done a good job in creating ripple in an otherwise unconscious vast multitudes of the rural poor about their rights for development and better quality of life.

Appendix 1

Physical and Financial Progress Under IRDP During 1987–88 Till January, 1988

(Rs. in lakhs)

Sl. No.	*Name of the States/UT*	*Total Allocation*	*Central Share*	*Central release*	*State release*	*Utilisation*
1	*2*	*3*	*4*	*5*	*6*	*7*
1.	Andhra Pradesh	4347.72	2173.86	2172.26	1086.98*	4167.59
2.	Arunachal Pradesh	384.00	384.00	187.04	–	127.76
3.	Assam	1365.16	682.58	519.01	341.70[4]	1047.19*
4.	Bihar	8410.68	4205.34	2974.51	2245.95	6794.50
5.	Goa	80.00	80.00	48.00	–	60.90
6.	Gujarat	2123.03	1061.51	1016.04	795.75$	1850.62
7.	Haryana	673.45	336.73	486.73	336.73	644.73
8.	Himachal Pradesh	385.76	192.88	177.88	99.39	474.27
9.	Jammu & Kashmir	606.14	303.07	194.85	–[4]	374.47[4]
10.	Karnataka	2593.47	1296.73	1028.87	648.37*	1576.56
11.	Kerala	1635.49	817.74	652.99	408.91	1347.51
12.	Madhya Pradesh	5851.95	2925.98	2432.67	1730.72*	4093.84
13.	Maharashtra	4424.25	2212.12	1923.92	1890.21	3238.88
14.	Manipur	129.14	64.57	37.42	60.00	118.06
15.	Meghalaya	192.96	96.48	65.87*	68.38	80.20*
16.	Mizoram	160.00	160.00	160.00	–	193.88
17.	Nagaland	168.00	84.00	177.90	139.18	203.03
18.	Orissa	3244.50	1622.25	1359.80	1053.36	2335.62
19.	Punjab	728.95	364.48	357.33	357.33	779.48
20.	Rajasthan	2879.05	1439.53	1249.49	943.40	2248.98
21.	Sikkim	32.00	16.00	21.00	10.05	27.37
22.	Tamil Nadu	4234.50	2117.25	1928.68	1642.10	3204.09
23.	Tripura	153.12	76.56	271.27	296.00	367.27
24.	Uttar Pradesh	11651.58	5825.79	5168.86	3874.73	9368.79
25.	West Bangal	4725.10	2362.55	2263.04	1275.46*	2934.25
26.	A & N Islands	40.00	40.00	20.00	–	16.96[4]
27.	Chandigarh	0.75	0.75	0.38	–	–
28.	D & N Haveli	8.00	8.00	5.18	–	7.97
29.	Delhi	40.00	40.00	40.00	–	35.17
30.	Daman & Diu	16.00	16.00	8.00	–	5.88
31.	Lakshadweep	21.25	21.25	–	–	14.03
32.	Pondicherry	32.00	32.00	62.00	–	28.59

Appndix 2

(Rs. in lakhs)

Sl. No.	*Name of the States/Uts*	*Annual target*	*Total families assisted*	*SC*	*ST*	*Women*
1	*2*	*3*	*4*	*5*	*6*	*7*
1.	Andhra Pradesh	273909	20495	77993	23871	38258
2.	Arunachal Pradesh	18860	3847	-	3847	529*
3.	Assam	81256	41120	3023	9555	4176*
4.	Bihar	536427	446570	116666	59925	51860
5.	Goa	5210	4000	188	19	1910
6.	Gujarat	147421	115219	14117	32600	30091
7.	Haryana	49438	33463	11498	-	11951
8.	Himachal Pradesh	27930	26162	13948	2401	5432
9.	Jammu & Kashmir	37745	17002	1517	-	1026[4]
10.	Karnataka	161239	90747	19849	2674	18985
11.	Kerala	115419	81138	22541	1810	26969
12.	Madhya Pradesh	384078	286580	53883	79037*	21167*
13.	Maharashtra	276970	187733	43822	26147	33295
14.	Manipur	7741	4750	-	3296	1325
15.	Meghalaya	9718	1232	-	1232	516*
16.	Mizoram	7368	2783	-	2783	901
17.	Nagaland	10720	3724	-	3724	638
18.	Orissa	208680	153025	35423	39300	18852
19.	Punjab	55158	45172	28932	-	10475
20.	Rajasthan	198162	155614	45889	27647	18660
21.	Sikkim	2017	1526	58	491	241
22.	Tamil Nadu	269380	201356	88942	2526	62144
23.	Tripura	10662	14624	1944	4752	496
24.	Uttar Pradesh	766063	590084	277206	1656	87017
25.	West Bangal	239674	184623	48346	8740	34054
26.	A & N Islands	1640	1448	-	121[4]	103[4]
27.	Chandigarh	60	12	2	-	5
28.	D & N Haveli	445	366	10	348	59
29.	Delhi	3038	1920	608	-	678
30.	Daman & Diu	1042	405	8	99	146
31.	Lakshadweep	900	265	-	265	103
32.	Pondicherry	2280	1107	397	-	431
	All India	3910650	2902412	906740	338866	482493

Appendix 3

(Rs. in lakhs)

Sl. No.	*Name of the States/UTs*	*Term Credit disbursed By Co-op. Banks*	*By Comml. Banks*	*Total*	*Progress till month*
1	*2*	*3*	*4*	*5*	*6*
1.	Andhra Pradesh	782.66	5882.52	6665.18	Jan. 88
2.	Arunachal Pradesh	4.02*	3.93*	8.14	Jan. 88
3.	Assam	56.39$	776.62$	133.03*	Jan. 88
4.	Bihar	566.84	11254.23	11820.07	Jan. 88
5.	Goa	1.28*	137.66*	147.53	Jan. 88
6.	Gujarat	128.86$	1307.39$	2386.29	Jan. 88
7.	Haryana	3.57	1031.29	1034.86	Jan. 88
8.	Himachal Pradesh	0.13	622.19	622.32	Jan. 88
9.	Jammu & Kashmir	147.13	407.40	602.66[4]	Dec. 87
10.	Karnataka	99.46*	2413.25*	2863.00	Jan. 88
11.	Kerala	334.47	2189.94	2524.21	Dec. 87
12.	Madhya Pradesh	810.44*	6261.27*	7765.67	Jan. 98
13.	Maharashtra	1099.18	4886.22	5985.40	Jan. 88
14.	Manipur	0.66	16.81	17.43	Jan. 88
15.	Maghalaya	7.08	6.93	14.01*	Jan. 88
16.	Mizoram	–	–	–	Dec. 87
17.	Nagaland	23.95	58.52	82.47	Jan. 88
18.	Orissa	224.15	2103.20	2347.35	Jan. 88
19.	Punjab	1.98	1663.09	1665.07	Jan. 88
20.	Rajasthan	346.63	2411.93	2758.56	Jan. 88
21.	Sikkim	1.08	43.91	44.99	Jan. 88
22.	Tamil Nadu	1811.94	4057.80	5869.74	Jan. 88
23.	Tripura	37.01	480.95	517.96	Jan. 88
24.	Uttar Pradesh	2386.70	13429.05	15815.74	Jan. 88
25.	West Bengal	236.03*	4823.16*	5260.45	Jan. 88
26.	A & N Islands	5.25[4]	24.46[4]	29.71[4]	Jan. 88
27.	Chandigarh	0.05$	–$	0.05$	Nov. 87
28.	D & N Haveli	1.11	11.42	12.53	Jan. 88
29.	Delhi	–	73.34	73.34	Jan. 88
30.	Daman & Diu	0.40	15.64	16.04	Dec. 87
31.	Lakshadweep	–	10.97	10.97	Jan. 88
32.	Pondicherry	0.21	33.39	33.60	Jan. 88
	All India	9438.66	66438.48	78328.38	

* – Information till December, 1987; 4 – Information till Nov., 1987

4 – Information till November, 1987

$ – Information till October, 1987; (–) – Nil

Notes and References

1. Indira Hirway, Reshaping IRDP, Economic and Political Weekly, June 25, 1988, p. A-95.
2. Lok Sabha Secretariat, Ninety-First Report, Public Accounts Committee (1986-87), Integrated Rural Development Programmes, New Delhi, 1987.
3. D. Bandyopadhyay, Direct Intervention Programmes for Poverty Alleviation, Economic and Political Weekly, 25th June, 1988, page. A-87.
4. C.H. Hanumantha Rao, Efficiency of Investment in IRDP, A Study of Uttar Pradesh, Economic and Political Weekly, 25th June, 1988, page A-25.
5. M.L. Dantwala, Poverty Alleviation Programme: Reconsideration, National Seminar on Poverty Alleviation Programmes, February 12,1988. Department of Rural Development, Ministry of Agriculture, New Delhi, page 78.
6. N.J. Kurian, IRDP, How relevant is it? Economic and Political Weekly, 26th December, 1987.

11

Problems of Entrepreneurship Development in Kumaun, Uttar Pradesh (An Empirical Investigation)*

SHOBHAN SINGH KHANKA**

Purpose of this Study

Of late, entrepreneurship has been considered as one of the important determinants of the industrial development and, in turn, economic development of an economy. Differences in the levels of entrepreneurship development between economies are, therefore, accounted for differences in their levels of industrial and economic development. However, the nature and degree of the entrepreneurship development and also its contribution to economic development are bound to vary from economy to economy depending upon their varying industrial climate, material resources, topography and the responsiveness of the government to the entrepreneurial growth. The varied trends of entrepreneurial growth in economies such as America, Japan, France and India support this trends, for example. Although the function of entrepreneurship is important in both developed and under-developed economies, nevertheless its role is more crucial in under-developed economies having limited and utilized resources. In this context, India presents a typical case of its own kind.

In India, efforts have been made from time to time to develop entrepreneurship in every region of the country to bring it in the main-

*The paper arouse out of a study entitled "Entrepreneurship in Small Scale Industries", financed by the University Grants Commission, New Delhi and carried out at the Department of Commerce, Kumaun, University, Nainital.
University, Nainital.

**Department of Commerce, Kumaon University, Nainital 263 002, Uttar Pradesh.

stream of economic development. Realising the fulcrum role of industrial development in the overall economic development of the hill region of Uttar Pradesh[7], the Draft Seventh Five Year Plan of Uttar Pradesh proposed an outlay of Rs. 80 crores on the industrial sector in the hill region of the State. Out of this, Rs. 40 crores is proposed for large and medium industries, Rs. 34 crores for small scale and village industries and Rs. 6 crores for geology and mining. During the Sixth Five Year Plan 1980-85, the outlay on industries in the hill region was Rs. 36.16 crores. However, in Proportion to the total plan outlays, the share of industries account for 6.34 per cent and 4.64 per cent respectively in the Sixth and Seventh Five Year Plans.

Kumaun division in Uttar Pradesh consisting of the three districts, viz., Almora, Pithoragarh and Nainital, represents one such special paradigm where several incentives and concessions are provided by the government to the entrepreneurs to establish industries there. The entrepreneurs look these facilities like green pastures from a distant plate. No matter that they found the same to be really thorny. Despite the various efforts made by the government, the fact remains that there does not seem any perceptible dent in the entrepreneurial front and, in turn, economic front of the division. The division seems lying where it was. What is particularly disheartening to mention is that the unhappy example displayed by the closure of several promising new industrial units especially in the hills, such as Kumar Bronze Ltd. and Madhukar Kagaj Udyog, Tarikhet has given increasing substance to the general feeling among the people and industrialisation holds no promise for them or for the area as well. It seems that this has led to a suspicion of outsiders and even local fly-by- night entrepreneurs to establish industries in the hills. In such dilemma, the need of a perspicacious investigation into the matter is obvious to locate the problems of industrial development so that therapeutic measures could be evolved for solving them. The present study endeavours to make a modest contribution in investigating into the specific problems of entrepreneurship development in Kumaun division of Uttar Pradesh.

Data Base And Methodology

The present study is exclusively based on the primary data collected through a sample survey of small entrepreneurs. Two industrial centre—Almora, i.e. Hills and Haldwani, i.e. Plains — were deliberately selected for survey purpose with a view to represent the two places — Hills and Plains — with their varied socio-economic backgrounds. After obtaining the up to-date lists of the registered units located in these two centres from the District Industry Centres, two criteria were formulated to satisfy an entrepreneur's inclusion in the sample survey. These criteria were:(i) the unit must be manufacturing unit, therefore, repair and other service shops were not included in the sample, (ii) The entrepreneurs must be the first generation entrepreneur. Thus, the entrepreneurs who were just managing the ancestral units have been excluded from the study. In this way, the entrepreneurs who satisfied these two criteria turned out 80-34 in Almora and 46 in Haldwani. Finally, a total of 50 entrepreneurs (62.50 per cent) of the total population—22 in Almora and 28 in Haldwani—were selected for survey work. A well structured questionnaire was prepared at the enterprise level and was put to these 50 entrepreneurs during January-February 1988. The sample size has been mainly subject to time and money at the disposal of the researcher.

Specific Problems of Entrepreneurship Development

The present study proposes to delve into the specific problems which entrepreneeurs have to contend with. The problems discussed here relate to specific aspects of entrepreneurship development such as raw material, marketing, finance, promotional procedures and others.

For this purpose, the entrepreneurs were asked to state the specific problems that they are facing in developing their units. While processing the data, we noticed that some entrepreneurs reported only one problem while others counted more than one problem in developing their units. Admittedly, an entrepreneur reporting one problem cannot be regarded at par with an entrepreneur stating more than one such problem for developing their units. It is difficult, if not impossible, for us to categorise them into types. Therefore, in order to regard all the entrepreneurs at par, only the most crucial problem was taken into consideration in all cases. What it signifies is that the one specific problem might have been regarded by the entrepreneurs as of prime importance in developing their units. The distribution of such entrepreneurs on the basis of their specific problems is presented in Table 1.

Table 1

Specific Problem of Entrepreneurship Development in Kumaun

Specific problems	*No. of entrepreneurs*					
	Hills		*Plains*		*Total*	
Raw material	11	(61.10)	11	(47.62)	21	(53.83)
Market	3	(16.67)	5	(23.81)	8	(20.51)
Finance	2	(11.11)	3	(14.29)	5	(12.82)
Infrastructural Facilities	1	(5.56)			1	(2.57)
Skilled labour			1	(4.76)	1	(2.57)
Promotional Procedures	1	(5.56)	1	(4.76)	2	(5.13)
Any other			1	(4.76)	1	(2.57)
Total	18	(100.00)	21	(100.00)	39	(100.00)

N.B. : Figures in parentheses denote percentage to the total.

(a) *Problems Connected with Procuring of Raw Material*

Among the problems of entrepreneurship development, the problem of raw material has emerged as one of the most serious one in developing entrepreneurship in our sample units as more than 50 per cent (21 entrepreneurs out of a total of 39) entrepreneurs stated this problem. Broadly speaking, in the absence of raw material, neither any enterprise can be established nor an entrepreneur can be emerged. It is important to mention that the problem of raw material seem both complex as well as numerous. Alongwith non-availability of raw-material are other equally important aspects pertaining to allied matters, for example, lack of finance for making required purchase, non-availability of quality raw materials, high market rates, dearth of infrastructural facilities like transportation. The fact remains the most of these problems are interlinked with one other. The one leads to the other and vice versa. Such inter-dependence makes it well- high impossible to affirm as to which one of the problems is really more serious and which one of minor significance. Yes, if one views merely by numerical order of the units stating incidence of individual problems, shortage of raw material appears to be the most serious problem in the regard. Two industry groups, namely, Biroza, Turpentine oil and Varnish and Woolen textile are specially plagued by the shortage of raw material, not to speak of quality raw material.

In earlier years, when there were dense and huge forests especially pine forests in the Kumaun hills, *lisa* was the main activity of the hill people. But, with the forest depletion over years, this activity has ceased to be main activity in the hills. Not only the production of *lisa* has fallen short of, but also had led to closure of several biroza units. At present, the *lisa* is made available to the units on the quota system by the government which has fallen for short of demand of the units. As a result, all the Biroza units in the region are facing an acute problem of *lisa*. This can best be gauged by the statement made by the entrepreneur himself in this regard.

The entrepreneurs of Laxmi Biroza Udyog, Chitai, Almora (1963), i.e. the oldest biroza unit in the Kumaun, affirmed that due to the very low availability of *lisa*, his unit works an average 15 days in a year. He stated that the unit can make use of 40 qts. lisa/day/8 hr. shift and, thus, requires about 12,000 qts. lisa annually. But, the irony of the fact is that the unit is made available 293 qts. *lisa* only during the preceding year 1987. Say, only 2.44 per cent of the units's *lisa* requirement was made available. This, thus, gives clue to understand the gross under-utilisation of the unit's production capacity due to dearth of raw material. Added to this is the timely delivery of whatever *lisa* sanctioned. Out of this meagre allotment of *lisa*, the wastage of a sizeable quantum of *lisa* is reported yet another problem, however. Putting the distillation formula forward, it was equated that the distillation of 100 qts. *lisa* products 75 qts. biroza and 15 qts. turpentine oil. Thus, 10 qts. (10.00 per cent) *lisa* is wasted in distilling process. By and large, similar stories of problem of procuring lisa were repeatedly narrated by all the biroza units covered in the present study.

Woolen textile industries are concentrated in a few locations in the Kumaun where the Bhotia Community is in sizeable number as they were the traditionally skilled carrying out the woolen industry especially carpet weaving industry. But, this industry has gradually languished over time mainly due to the non-availability of raw material, i.e. wool. In earlier years, these industries used to get most of their wool requirements either from Tibet or from their own sheep which they also use for carrying the articles they traded. But, with the cessation of Indo-Tibetan trade in 1962, not only the import of wool has discontinued and trading activity has ceased to be their main activity, but the Bhotias' interest in rearing sheep has also declined[2]. This has, in turn, posed an acute problem of wool for woolen textile industries in woolen textile industries in the region. Therefore, most of the wool required by them has to be procured from other sources and places which have not been found easy and economical by them. At present, most of the units get wool from quite distant places like Ludhiana and Panipat which claims a lot of transportation cost, waiting cost, etc.

(b) *Marketing*

Broadly speaking, if the proof of pudding lies in eating, the proof of all production lies in consumption/marketing. In fact, the goods have no value for the manufacturers unless these are sold. That is why marketing of goods has been regarded as an important aspect of the entrepreneurial performance. Let us turn our attention to find out the marketing aspect of the industries covered in the present study. It is seen from Table 1 that after raw material, problems of marketing have been reported the second major problem of the entrepreneurial development. Even more than one-fifth of the entrepreneurs reported the problems of marketing their products. As regards the problems of marketing, three reasons were enumerated in main:

First, especially the handicrafts industries like carpet weaving and copper works complained their severe competition with the modern products of the medium and large scale industries. Several factors have contributed to aggravate the marketing competition between the two. There is an implicit assumption of poor quality for goods manufactured in the small sector. Of course, the traditional hallmarks of the small scale industries are slowly, yet steadily, changing. These need to cater to wide diversity and changing tastes and preferences of their clientele which they do fail.

Advertisement of the products seems yet another factor increasing the competition between the two sectors. It has become fashionable, particularly in the case of medium and large scale industries, to advertise their products through the elaborate sales-promotion methods such as cadres of trained salesmen, advertisement in cinema slides, posters, papers, magazines and so on. On the contrary, small scale industries lack in the required resources as well as knowledge to practice the methods of sales promotion. As a result, the former usually have patented-nanus which facilitate the dealers in selling the products without making any painstaking efforts. In such case, it can also be postulated that in the case of the products of small scale industries, at least at the initial stage, persuasive capacity of the dealer plays an important role in influencing their sales. Inevitably, the dealers, demand and the producers are bound to pay a relatively higher rate of commission than those paid by the large scale producers. This leads to an increase in their unit cost and, thus, impinges on their capacity to compete with the large sector. Besides, the lion's share of the margin of profits also goes to these dealers. These factors taken together have a direct bearing on their competitive ability with the large sector.

Second, that the changing demand of the industries previously demanding the products of ancillary units is yet another serious problem of marketing for the latter is brought into light by our field investigation. For example, Ranibagh Packing Industries, Ranibagh was established with a view to fulfil the packing case requirements of the Hindustan Machines Tools (Watch Factory V) Ltd., Ranibagh for which the HMT made a promise also. But, as the entrepreneur incisively dogmatized, the HMT has been purchasing the packing cases for somewhere else, i.e. Bareilly. Bhawani Plastic Industries, Gora Paraw (Haldwani) illustrates yet another similar case of so created market problem. It was initially started to supply plastic containers to the Soyabeen Factory, Halduchorh (Haldwani), which did so for one year also. Later, the Soyabeen Factory substituted plastic containers by polythene bags, thus, creating dearth of demand for the Plastic Industry. Evidently, the industry has come to a grinding halt due to the gross lock of demand for its products, i.e. containers.

Likewise, Kapoor Industries, Ranibagh presents one classical case which, instead of the Government's standing instructions to the Indenting Officers belonging to the hill districts of Kumaun and Garhwal divisions to make purchases of phenyle from this industry[3], has been starving of getting orders for its produce. When asked the entrepreneur why did the divisional Indenting Officers do not place order to him, he referred to the rate of commission providing an inkling, however rough, of which less said is better. This dilemma underlines the policy implications in this regard.

Third, particularly in the case of handicrafts such as copper works and carpet weaving, it was noticed that the price realised is usually better when the sales are made at the place of production itself than when these products are marketed in fairs. It looks that, very possibly, the manufacturers are in a better bargaining position at home than in other locations like fairs where they take their products for selling.

A few units also found experiencing the practice of sales at pre-determined prices. Such sales were noticed more frequent to intermediary agencies. By investigating one step further, it was noticed that in such sales the prices are pre-determined by the intermediaries much earlier than the actual time of manufacture, mainly in consideration of financial accommodations granted or raw material supplied or again for any other so-called favours received. Sale of products at pre-determined prices among the small scale units is indicative of their financial vulnerability, inter alia. Besides, it is also suggestive of the fact that the lion's share of the margin of profits is also usurped by these intermediaries.

Lastly, the practice of credit sales was also found common in some industries. The duration of credit reported was quite higher even for more than one year. One sure conclusion that one can draw from credit sales is that it drains the units of their already meagre working capital, thus, keeps them idle and inhibits their development.

(c) *Problems of Procuring Capital*

Realising the lubricious role of finance in production process, what concerns us in this section is the problems of finance encountered by the entrepreneurs covered in the present investigation. As could be seen from Table 1, out of the 39 entrepreneurs, 5 (12.82 per cent) reported the problems of procuring required capital as their most serious problem in the development of their entrepreneurs. It is important to mention that the problems of procuring capital are both quantitative and qualitative.

It is a widely-held belief that the small entrepreneurs lack in their own capital and, therefore, largely depend upon the institutional finance for their capital requirements. This is well reflected in their very high debt-equity ratio. In practice, the institutional long-term finances are given mainly for the purpose for acquiring fixed assets such as plant and machinery, construction of sheds and creating for other fixed assets. As per rules, such assistance cannot be diverted towards working capital resources. In fact, the problem of capital faced by the entrepreneurs is of working capital not of fixed capital. Of course, financial agencies/institutions are there which provide working capital to the small scale units under certain rules and regulations which, as affirmed by the entrepreneurs, often falls short of their requirements. The following Table 2 gives an inkling of the magnitude of differences between the capital asked and the sanctioned.

Table 2

Percentage Difference between the Financial Assistance asked by the Entrepreneurs and Released by the Financial Institutions

Difference	*No. of Entrepreneurs*	*Percentage*
No difference	15	35.71
0–10	2	4.76
11–20	9	21.43
21–30	7	16.67
31–40	7	16.67
41–50	2	4.76

N.B. :Here, the entrepreneuers refer to all reporting the problem of procuring capital. No matter, the problem is serious or otherwise.

The entrepreneurs who are encountering the problem of capital ascribed blame on commercial banks for their reluctance to provide working capital. Another problem attributed vicariously to the banks was the time-lag between request for financial requirements made and the actual receipt of the same which is invariably protracted. To quote an instance, Uttar Pradesh Finance Corporation (UPFC) sanctioned Rs. 7.53 lakhs for Kalika Wood Works, Ranikhet in 1974. First disbursement of Rs. 2.17 lakhs was made in November, 1976 whereas the factory had already gone into production in March, 1975. Not only that, later on the UPFC cancelled sanction for as much Rs. 4.83 lakhs. A project involving in the manufacture of Nuts and Bolts at Ranikhet presents their typical case of such kind which was declared eligible for rehabilitation finance in 1982 but the working capital facility was provided to it only in 1986. Usually, this refers to the financial agencies.Then what happens is that finance is not obtained when it is most wanted. Since the government/financial agencies take much time in disbursing the funds, the entrepreneurs have to obtain bridging loans during the intervening period and, thus, they have to pay interest not only in loans but also on subsidy. Let some more facts speak first.

Sanjay Udyog, Almora (established in 1983), manufacturer of controlled copies, applied for working capital for Rs. 25,000 to State Bank of India, Almora in 1982 and was sanctioned Rs. 15,000 only in 1984, i.e. after one year of installing machinery. The entrepreneur further affirmed that the protracted release of funds caused the unit a loss of Rs. 11,000 before starting production[4].

That the small entrepreneurs encounter problems not only of less and delayed finance from the financial agencies but yet another problems as well as brought into light by Hillman Video Industries, Almora (established in1982). After releasing Rs. 4.3 lac funds as against Rs. 60 lac asked the Nainital Bank Ltd., Almora stopped further releasing of funds to the industry and, the entrepreneur stated, filed suit in the High Court against the unit for financial matters.

It was also complained by some entrepreneurs that financial assistances are not provided to the needy units but to those who have good report with the financial agencies. Mr. Hira Lal Tamta, Almora, a copper artisan and the winner of the national awards for his excellent artisanship opined vicariously, by alluding to his neighbouring artisan, that "in practice, the government helps to those who do not work and, thus, are not needy and deprives them of who really do work and are really needy for the government helps such as financial assistance like me". He summed up by starting 'all know this dilemma of which less said is better'.

In order to find out who is really at fault, we held discussions with the bank authorities also. The discussion revealed that the bank too face certain difficulties in financing the small industries working capital requirements. The bank consider the small scale units as 'uncreditworthy' because of the restrictions of the Reserve Bank of India and the inability of the small entrepreneurs to comply with the loan provisions. The obvious reason being the inability on the part of these small entrepreneurs to provide sound securities, collateral and the uncertain demand conditions for their products. Yet, it does not mean that the banks are not providing finance to the small scale industries. Thus, it seems difficult, if not impossible, to judge who is really at fault-bank or industry itself.

In such dilemma, the dominance of the unorganised private sources is inevitable to figure the capital scene with all the unpalatable aspects associated with them such as rather high, if not exorbitant, rate of interest.

In practice, the pausity of working capital in any industry may be either due to blockage of funds in procuring raw material, piling up of unsold stock, wrong credit policy of all. As regard the first two, none of the industries reported heavy blockage of funds in raw materials and finished stock and thus, were not exactly the sources of the problem of liquid resources. In fact, the wrong credit policy, i.e. high debtor-creditor ratio, was found to be the main reason for creating problem of working capital.

Table 3

Credit Facilities Extended and Received

Credit	*Credit Facilities*			
	Extended to the customers		*Received from the suppliers*	
	No.	*Percentage*	*No.*	*Percentage*
No	36	72	23	46
Yes	14	28	27	54
Total	50	100	50	100

As can be seen from Table 3 that only 46 per cent of the entrepreneurs are getting credit facilities from their suppliers but 72 per cent of them have to extend credit facilities to their customers. It only reflects the financial vulnerability of the small entrepreneurs. Thus, the origin of the liquid resource problem to a great extent, has been traced to the wrong credit policy practiced by the small scale industries.

(d) *Procedural Delays by Promotional Authorities*

While analysing the entrepreneurial performance, one seldom overlooks to discuss the time taken in completing promotional formalities. Howerver, 5.13 per cent of the entrepreneurs of our sample (see Table 1) stated procedural delays in promoting their industries as their specific problem. The entrepreneurs reported that right from the genesis of an idea upto the establishment of an enterprise, the completion of promotional formalities, says, 'gestation period' took more than reasonable time. If we look at the various reasons for delays in completing promotional formalities given in Table 4, as reported by the entrepreneurs themselves, it gives an inkling of intensity of procedural delays in this regard.

Table 4

Reasons for Delays in Completing Promotional Formalities

Reasons for Delays	*No. of the Formalities*	*Percentage*
Procedural delays in office	25	78.13
Formalities of finance	1	3.12
Procurement of Plant & Machinery	1	3.12
Procedural delays in Development agencies	1	3.12
Lack of capital	1	3.12
Cannot say	3	9.39
Total	3[illegible]	100.00

As is evident from Table 4 that nearly fourth-fifth of the entrepreneurs stated procedural delays in concerned offices for their delays in completing promotional formalities. It is observed that once an entrepreneur decides to set up a manufacturing unit, he has to interact with minimum of 20 to 26 agencies, depending on whether the unit involves foreign collaboration or export marketing, to make his/her unit an operating one[6]. Here, the procedural delays experienced by M/s Saraswati Woollen Mills (P) Ltd., Ranikhet, seem pertinent to quote. This mill was registered in 1973 and it got an industrial license two years later, it took about 9 years for it to build the factory shed, install the machinery and go into production. The evil effects of the procedural delays were seen in the cost escalation of the project from Rs. 32 lakhs in 1973 to Rs. 56 lakhs in 1981. While interrogating with the entrepreneurs, we were repeatedly told that the bureaucratic attitude of the promotional authorities has been one of the main reasons delaying the promotional stage. When asked them if the concerned authorities, in their opinion, deliberately linger the formalities to be completed, most of them replied in affirmative. They further alluded that those who have good rapport with the concerned officials and those who can grease their palms of which less said is better, may get formalities completed fairly quickly.

But, on the basis of our field experience gained and the discussions held with the officials involved in promotional activities, we came to know that the new entrepreneurs often submit unrealistic feasibility reports and incompleting their promotional formalities. Notwithstanding, it does not purport that there is no procedural delays on the part of those concerned authorities. Facts and figures confirm that there is definitely procedural delays, may be of less or more degree, on their part. At the same time, the promotional delays on the part of the entrepreneurs themselves is found mainly due to their non-awareness about the various promotional formalities to be completed through various departments and authorities. Be that as it may, the promotional authorities seem to be more at fault than the entrepreneurs themselves so as far as the procedural delays is concerned.

(e) *Other Problems*

The problems concerned with infrastructural facilities are reported by 1 (2.57 per cent) entrepreneur only who belonged to the hills. Absence of approach road and the protracted supply of power connection are cited as the main problems of this category. Out of the 39 units, again only 1 (2.57 per cent) stated the problem of skilled labour. However, it does not imply that the units employ the unskilled labour which like-elsewhere is found in abundant number in our region also. The reason is that most of the units firstly impart training to their employees in the particular line of activity to fulfil their labour requirements. In this way, the units do not face the problem of skilled labour they require.

Exceptionally, an industry namely, M/s Saraswati Woollen Mills (P) Ltd., Ranikhet producing shoddy woollen yarn cited the problem of the skilled weaver which the mill has been getting either from Panipat or Amritsar at a fairly higher scale of pay. Since these plains weavers are often unable to withstand the rugged climatic conditions of the hills, they happen to be the birds of passage for the industry. Thus, the industry remains without the required weaver during the intervening period even sometimes for 2-3 months. With its already jejune capital resources, it is an uneconomic proposition for the industry itself to impart training to produce only one weaver. Another problem of this industry observed is its poor management due to which the industry has been reeling under the penumbra of sickness for its very inception[7].

Last but not the least, although the government has notified all the three districts of Kumaun Division as Category 'A' districts of providing several concessions and incentives to the entrepreneurs for establishing industries there, many of the entrepreneurs were not availing these facilities mainly because of the complexities involved in their availment.

Here, it will be pertinent to note that only extra incentive given to the industrially backward hill areas consists of the transport subsidy. The other incentives are available to the hill region of Uttar Pradesh on the same basis as all other industrially backward areas in the country or the state as the case may be. As per the government's declaration, an industry established on July 31, 1971 and after in the division is entitled to 75 per cent subsidy on the cost of transporting raw material and finished goods from the nearest declared rail head to the location of the unit. However, at present facility of transport subsidy is Kanpur-based. The District Industry Centre (DIC), Almora reported that it is authorised to provide transport subsidy upto Rs. 20,000 per quarter and there is only one case as yet which enjoyed this facility from DIC, Almora, the case being that of Almora Magnesite Limited, Almora which is a large scale industry. Thus, none of the small scale industries has so far availed the facility of transport subsidy in the hills. This warrants further detailed investigations into the reasons why the entrepreneurs have not been availing various facilities like transport subsidy declared by the Government.

At the same time, if the tell-tale information and allusion stated by the local people are to be believed, surprisingly, even the intentions of the so called entrepreneurs are vested in doubt. The entrepreneurs set up industry only to take advantage of subsidies and incentives and are least interested in its viable running. One such vested purpose is solved, they pack up the industry. This again underlines the policy information in providing the incentive package to the entrepreneurs.

To sum up, it can be concluded that the various problems enlisted above are not at all comprehensive and exhaustive one. These are just illustrative of the general set of problems encountered by our sample industries in their development efforts. The study tautologically states problems of entrepreneurship development. For finding solutions, we leave it to the wiser minds.

Need of Manpower Planning for entrepreneurs Development

Having discussed the various problems faced by our sample units, one major question we address at the last is the need of manpower planning for entrepreneurship development in India, in general, and in a backward economy like Kumaun, in particular.

History bears evidence to the fact that economic development has been an outcome of effective utilization of both human and material resources. Nevertheless, it is unequivocally accepted that man stands at the centre of any economic activity because he assumes various roles in the production process, such as an organiser of human and material resources, worker, consumer and exchange agent. Out of these multiple roles, his role as an organiser of human and material resources, in an ultimate sense as an entrepreneur, is the most important and basic one.

In economic parlance, an entrepreneur is the person who tries to create something new, organises production, undertakes risks and handles economic uncertainty involved in the enterprise. Thus, entrepreneurship is a set of attributes which the entrepreneurs possess and which help them behave entrepreneurially. That is why there has not been a mushroom growth of the entrepreneurs in any society. It is these attributes that the entrepreneurs combines the land of the one, the labour of another and capital of yet another and, thus, produces a product. The fact remains that the pattern of entrepreneurship development determines the pace and shape of industrial development and, in turn, economic development of an economy. Thus, economic development has always been concommitant factor of entrepreneurship development.

It is an entrepreneur who firstly explores the development potentials whatever an economy had and then makes economic exploitation of the same. A cross-country examination evidences that the economies which have had enterprising manpower developed faster than which lacked these. To quote, in India, if one compares the Punjab and the Eastern Uttar Pradesh both inhabited simultaneously, he finds clue that it is the enterprising attitude of the Punjabis accounted for the Punjab's much higher economic development than the Eastern Uttar Pradesh which has still been reeling where it was many years ago. It is the achieving society of the Punjab due to which the Punjab could develop by leaps and bounds. Then, the question arises: if the people of the Eastern Uttar Pradesh, for example, cannot be made enterprising like that of Punjab so that the former could also be brought in the mainstream of development? In fact, the same underlines the need of manpower planning for entrepreneurship development to achieve higher levels of economic development in India, in general and, in underdeveloped regions like Eastern Uttar Pradesh and Kumaun, in particular.

However, the study does not propose to suggest measures how to develop the enterprising acumen in the society, or say, how to develop

entrepreneurship therein. Yet it can be said with certitude that, in the present times, the enterprising attitude has been no more an acumen which one gets from his very birth, but it is the acumen that can be inculcated by imparting necessary education and training to the prospective people. The late Establishment of some such institutions in the country like entrepreneurship Development Institute, Ahmedabad; National Institute of Entrepreneurship and Small Business Development, New Delhi' Institute of Entrepreneurship Development, Lucknow and the others are testimonies to affirm not only the need of manpower planning for entrepreneurship development but also the fact that the entrepreneurial acumen can be achieved by imparting necessary education and training.

Notes and References

1. Government of Uttar Pradesh, Planning Development: Draft Seventh Five Year Plan (1985-90) and Annual Plan 1985-86, Vol. I, Regional Sub-Plans, (I) Hill Region, Table 2, p. 6.
2. Papola, T.S., Production of Woollen Carpets in Kumaun and Garhwal, Giri Institute of Development Studies, Lucknow, 1980 (Mimeo), pp. 25-26.
3. Letter No. 4019-926/1985-86, dated October 1, 1985 from Shri O.N. Vaidhya, Commissioner, Kumaun Division, Nainital to all the Head of the Departments, Kumaun Division, Nainital.
4.

	Rs. Ps.
Depreciation	2,500.00
Unit Rent	3,600.00
Miscellaneous Expenses	2,500.00
Machine Interest	2,500.00
Total	11,100.00

5. Shetty, M.C., Small Scale and Household Industries in a Developing Economy, Asia Publishing House, Bombay, 1963, pp. 174-75.
6. Shivaramu, S., Entrepreneurship and Enterprise Growth, Seema Publications, Delhi, 1985, p. 21.
7. Joshi, B.K., Impact of Industrialisation on the Social Ecology of the Hill Areas of Uttar Pradesh, Giri Institute of Development Studies, Lucknow, 1978 (Mimeo.), p. 54.

12

The Role of Rural Industrialisation Towards Eradication of Rural Poverty : Case Study

R.B. SINGH*

The divorce of the countryside from industrial activity has led to an unbalanced rural economy solely dependent on agriculture. This need to be corrected by promoting appropriate and intermediate technologies aimed at 'production by the masses' rather than 'mass production, by few. Experience in developing countries testified to the close relationship between agricultural productivity and rural industrialisation. There is no doubt that rural industrialisation is an urgent necessity in developing societies like Siwan district as well as North Indian Plan. In the above context, the planning commission of the Government of India formulated Rural Industries Projects Programmes in different districts. Pressure on land in rural areas should be relieved by the provision of non-agricultural jobs in industries and services. It would actually mean the adoption of a more rational approach which involves the improvement of agricultural productivity, provision of employment to the entire workforce, increasing incomes of those living in rural areas in proportion to those in urban areas and the provision of urban facilities in rural areas.

Thus the industrial development in rural areas would have certainly included three major consequences.

(i) Management of traditional village artisans,

(ii) Development of major agro-industry like sugar,

(iii) Development of small-scale village and cottage industries.

The above schemes should preferably be small labour intensive technologies because of the unskilled labour in rural areas and scarce

* Department of Geography, University of Delhi.

foreign exchange in India. The goals of rural industry plan, therefore will be:

(i) to create income and employment opportunities other than in agricultural sector,

(ii) to make the rational use of locally available raw materials, labour, capital, skills and talents,

(iii) to produce variety of goods and commodities in processed or semi-processed forms,

(iv) to establish coordination between different sectors, and

(v) to divert the flow of labour and capital from towns to smaller service centres and villages.

The study area, Siwan District, lying in the north-western part of the Bihar state, covers an area of 2,223.0 km[4] and has population of 17,78,050 (1981). There area 1,436 inhabited and 105 uninhabited villages, and three towns, viz., Siwan, Maharajganj and Mairwa, comprising of 15 blocks.

Management of Traditional Village Artisans

There is a large number of traditional rural artisans working in the district. These are declining and are facing serious challenges as a consequence of urbanisation and modernisation process. These include carpenters, blacksmiths, goldsmiths, potters etc. In addition, cobblers, washermen, tailors, barbers and masons carry on their occupation in a traditional manner and they are least affected by changes in technology. Most of the artisans get employment from 75 to 175 days in a years and remain unemployed for rest of the year (Table 1). It is obvious that excepting the barbers, masons and cobblers, the other remained unemployed for a fair number of days.

From personal inquiry, it reveals that their incomes are meagre, and they are infavour of innovation and adoption of new implements to increase their income. Some expressed desire to get training and financial help to buy tools implements and raw material. The existing and proposed status of rural artisans have been shown in Table 1. Most of these artisans like blacksmiths, carpenters, potters, barbers and washermen are governed by Jajmani System[5]. They get cereals and cash for maintenance in some cases. It is evident that the district is frequently affected by flood and drought, as a result of which these artisans do not get their wages particularly at the time of crop harvesting. It is quite significant to raise the standard of living and way of life of the village artisans. Firstly, financial assistance to modernize the equipment and to establish the permanent shops and secondly, proper training programme should be provided to keep pace with the district industrial training centre.

Table 1

Transforming Traditional Structure of Rural Artisans

Name of artisan	*Existing Occupation*	*Suggestion for improvement*	*Existing employment days*
1	*2*	*3*	*4*
Blacksmith	Making kitchen utensils and implements small agricultural tools, building materials and keel	Modern machines like polishing electroplating and grinding	125
Cobbler	Making the cheaper type shoes and monts, repair of shoes part of rural music instrument	Good quality shoes and chappals; bags and belts, etc.	225
Carpenter	Making of wooden ploughs and other tools, bullock cart, part of building construction work, tile setters and domestic use materials.	Improving the quality of building fittings works, agro-implement and furniture	90
Barber	Usual job by moving from house to house, professional jobs at the time of ritual occasion	Changing style of hair-cutting in society concerned use of shaving cream and new tools	260

1	2	3	4
Potter	Earthern vessels for use in households flower vase, earthern lamp, plate, tumbler, small cup and different toys and domestic pots.	Making impervious pottery articles, tils for wall, roof, floor and artistic articles and bricks	80
Tailor	Old and out-dated technique and equipment for sewing	Adoption of new design for dresses preparation of ready-made garments	190
Mason	Traditional method for constructinon of houses	House construction by improved tools with scientific and environments consideration, construction of pucca streets.	250
Goldsmith	Small-scale traditional ornament making, repairing etc.	Attractive and different designs of ornament preparation	100
Washerman	Mostly washing by simple traditional method by Reh.	Use of chemicals (soaps and detergents) press etc.	270

Source: Personal Observation.

Development of Major Agro-Industry (Sugar) :

There is no large-scale industry in the district excepting sugar factories (New Sawan (Siwan) S.K.G. (Siwan) and the Bihar Sugar Works (Pachrukhi)). Pachrukhi factory was closed during 1975-76 due to the delay in bank loan, payment of wages of labourers and price to cane growers. Another sugar factory at Maharajganj has been closed for ever since more than one and half decades.

Every factory has some reserved area which normally supplies a considerable quantity of cane, Pachrukhi mill has the smallest area (153 villages). Besides this, 85 to 108 villages are being reserved for Pratappur Sugar Industries Limited which is situated in neighbouring district of U.P. and 204 villages are also being reserved for Bharat Sugar Works Limited, Sidhawalia (Gopalganj). Some other industries, located in neighbouring district like Harkhua and Mirganj (Gopalganj, Marhaurah (Saran) etc. are getting some sugarcane from time to time through its purchasing centres in Siwan district.

Production of the factory depends upon the crushed sugarcane obtained from the surrounding area. The full capacity in the district would together require about 36.50 lakh quintals. Per acre average yield is, presently, recorded to be near about 22 metric tons while average recovery of sugar is 8.5 to 9.5 kg out of 100 kg sugarcane due to mass adoption of local seeds. The quantities of sugarcane crushed, sugar production, recovery, working days, cane requirement, wages etc. by three factories during the two periods are given in Table 2. Gur is currently manufactured by the traditional process. Small units come up in the sugarcane growing areas and operate with poor milling machinery and traditional production techniques. The yield of gur is low and of poor quality.

The district sugar factories are suffering from the following main problems : (i) lack of source of adequate finance, (ii) short-fall in sugarcane acreage due to introduction of multiple cropping and provision of irrigation facilities, (iii) not enough good acreage in sugarcance due to soil texture and structure, (iv) lack of initiative on the part of sugar factory in cane development works, (v) lack of initiation of the modernizing the rehabiltation of plant machinery and (vi) higher cost of production of sugar and unremunerative price of sugar.

Table 2

Year wise Statistics of Sugar Factory

Name of variable	*Factory*					
	New Siwan		*S.K.G.*		*Pachrukhi*	
	1970–71	*1977–78*	*1970–71*	*1977–78*	*1970–71*	*1977–78*
1	*2*	*3*	*4*	*5*	*6*	*7*
Sugar cane area in hectares	6759.53	4471.73	2848.30	2794.70	5966.66	3773.58
Per acre average yield in metrictons	21.32	23	23.15	24	21.29	23
Actual cane crushed in lakh quintals	10.51	7.69	9.11	9.82	11.34	4.37
Sugar production quintals	97650	66626	20190	82927	102841	32673
Total number of working days	134	87	150	127	129	87
Average recovery in kg in 100 kg cane	9.14	8.75	8.8	8.62	9.07	7.46
Total number of villages severed	580		153		709	
Normal cane requirement in lakh quintals	12.30		9.99		14.30	
Wages of labour in lakhs of rupees per month	1.5		1.5			

Source: Distrct Sugar cane Development Reports

Management of By-product of Sugar Industry

There are three by-products of sugar refineries namely, bagasse, molasses and press-mud. Bagasse and molasses accounts 35% and 3%, respectively, as a consequence of sugar-cane crushed. And the rest constitutes press-mud. Press-mud is a compost fertilizer, which has large demand in the entire district where its cost is Rs. 4.50 per quintal approximately. Bagasses product, such as insulation boards, hard boards or news print can be established with the provision of cheap power supply. It is noted that failure of power supply interrupt the functioning of sugar factories, resulting in the less production. Arrangement of equally cheap alternative fuel like thermal power is most important, because, continued power supply will increase the production and provide more employment opportunity. Molasses is mainly used for manufacture of alcohol. A plant is to be set up to utilize the molasses near the sugar factories of Siwan adjacent to the sugar industry would be the utilisation of sugar for processing into pharmaceutical products mainly Sarbital, Ascorbic acid and Riboflavin. These products will promote the growth of the drug plants in the region, a part of molasses should be used for manufacturing good yeast which is a good source of protein. Yeast is valuable for human consumption and is used in pharmaceutical industry, bakeries, etc.

Small Scale Village and Cottage Industries

Existing Small-scale Industrial Structure and Growth

The growth of industries in the district during last two decades was slow. It is evident that in 1969, there were only 20 registered small-scale industries, which is an indication of very poor economic condition of the district. Formation of Siwan subdivision as district in 1974 has led to rapid progress in industrial activities. As a consequence of establishment of district Industry Centre, Incentive to industrial units has grown in different blocks. The industrial units increased to 159 in 1975, 234 in 1977 and 368 in 1979. In addition, there were 118 unregistered industrial units, according to the survey report of Lead-bank.

Another Limitation which is distinctive to the Siwan district, is the extremely uneven distribution of industrial activity between the small market centres to towns. Large-scale industry like sugar preferably be located in or near the cities or towns to obtain their markets, reserves of skilled labour, power supplies, etc. But the small industrial activities are also basically localized at the district headquarters-Siwan (51%) and the remaining (21%) in the rest of the two towns, Maharajganj and Mairwa. Other 8%, 5% and 3% are respectively in nearest block headquarters Packrukhi, Hussainganj and Andar. The remaining industry (12%) is mostly located in 9 other blocks headquarters far away from Siwan which does not receive proper benefit (see Table 3).

To find out the disparities in industrial activities deviation indices have been calculated by the following method:

$$I_i = \frac{(X+Y)}{2}$$

in which I_i = Industrial intensity, X = ratio of number of units in a block to the district, Y ratio of number of employment in a block to the district, within above perspectives, there appears wide spatial gaps between Siwan (0.4) and Siwan (7.36) blocks. Majority of units are concentrated in Siwan blocks, particularly in Siwan towns. Deviation index of four blocks (3 having towns and Pachrukhi) is recorded as more than 1.10, while for the 10 blocks it comes to below 0.70; and one block have 0.70-1.10 (Table 3).

The Strategy for the Development of Small scale Industries

District employment statistics shows the 5,507 persons were registered unemployed in June 1978 of which about 1,700 have passed some technical training or skills. The statistics do not give real picture of rural unemployed. Nevertheless, majority of the population who are young, living in rural areas, in the employable age-group of 15-54 are unemployed. These persons are educated and therefore comprise a potential human resource to the district. This problem of unemployment, however, can be solved by rural industrialization to a greater extent.

Table 3

Siwan District Industrial Intensity

Block	*Total Units*	*Industrial intensity*	
		%	*Deviation Index*
1	2	*3*	*4*
Siwan	190	49.06	7.36
Hussain ganj	17	5.63	0.84
Andar	12	4.21	0.63
Darauli	5	1.25	0.17
Guthni	3	0.71	0.11
Mairwa	34	8.49	1.27
Barharia	3	0.77	0.12
Panchrukhi	31	7.39	1.11
Goriakothi	3	0.82	0.12
Basantpur	5	1.20	0.18

1	2	*3*	*4*
Bhagwanpur	8	2.02	0.30
Maharajganj	45	15.62	2.34
Daraundha	6	1.59	0.24
Siswan	1	0.25	0.04
Raghunathpur	5	1.09	0.16
Total District	368	6.67	(Dist. Mean (-1)

Source: District Industry Office Report.

To improve the state of the rural population, it is necessary not only to increase agricultural productivity but also to introduce first off all agro-processing and agro-supporting small industries as well as improving the techniques and technologies of the household industries. These industries would contribute rapidly to the improvement of rural population, rural income, and rural standard of living. Previously many planners were infact, quite hostile to the idea of small scale plants and so called rural industries. Any glorification of rural industrialization or of handicrafts as a panacea of development of under-developed areas must be recognised as a utopian dream. But the district which has agricultural economy requires provision of small industries which ensures their quick success in the development of rural economy.

Table 4

Proposed Small Scale Industry

Name of Unit	*Raw material*	*Existing problem*	*No. of Proposed*	*Employment potential*	*Per unit in thousand*
1	2	*3*	*4*	5	*6*
Gur and Khandsari	Sugarcane	Crude and uneconomical methods leads to waste in yield quality dirtiness	30	120	25
Agricultural implement	Wood, iron and steel	Traditionally made wooden horrows plows,	15	60	
Rice Mill	Rice	Inadequate mills	15	30	7
Flour Mill	Wheat	- Do -	15	30	7
Dal Mill	Pulses	- Do -	5	15	45

1	2	3	4	5	6
Oil ghani	Oilseeds	Inadequate and indigenous type of Kholu	300	300	22
Bakery	Maida, wheat, flourmilk, sugaroil	Small and inadequate unit, lack of dairy products	5	35	48
Packing cases	Bamboo basket	Undurable heavy weight preparation, wastage and spoilage	10	190	88
Polythene bags	Pulp, polythene	Inadequate	3	12	2
Lead cups and plates	Dry leaves	Traditionally making Dona and Pattal	15	60	3
Bone meal unit	Animal bones	Only used for cattle, poultry, pig feed	3	12	121
Readymade garment	Plastic, stone, thread	Inadequate and unsuitable design	15	90	50
Leather industry	Animal skin	Unskilled crafts	30	180	16
Handloom	Local cotton	Mainly chaders, dhotis towels and shirting made by old and outdated tools, lack of credit, training and marketing	360	1080	16
Manufacturing of brick	Earthern soils	Inadequate due to heavy demand for road, well, canal, dam and house construction	15	300	14

1	*2*	*3*	*4*	*5*	*6*
Cementhume pipes	**Cement**	**Requirement for pipe culverts and water supply lines**	**2**	**-**	**320**
Wood processing unit, saw mill	**Wood timber**	**Heavy demand of wooden furniture and agro-implements lack of unit plywood work**	**10**	**100**	**150**
Washing soap unit	**Oil, fat and stone powder**	**Lack of the unit, plywood work**	**15**	**45**	**22**
Safety match factory	**Soft wood and chemical**	**Lack of unit**	**3**	**-**	**300**
Exercise book and book binding	**Paper, printing and pulp**	**Inadequate unit**	**15**	**75**	**16**
Automobile repair	**Parts, skill**	**Demand with vehicular traffic growth**	**30**	**180**	**45**
Bee keeping	**Plants of vegetable orchard, oil seeds**	**Traditional method and wastage**	**600**	**600**	**2**
Coldstorage	**Agricultural products, potato**	**Inadequate**	**1**	**15**	**900**
Nuts and bolts manufacturing unit	**Iron & steel**	**Inadequate**	**10**	**100**	**72**
Gobar gas plant	**Animal dung**	**Fuel shortage can fulfilled**	**70**	**70**	**3**

Source: Basedon Lead Bank Survey Reports and Personal Observation.

Table 4 shows the proposed small scale unit with raw material, per unit cost, employment potential in the context of local resources and needs available in the district. It is aimed to convert agricultural communities into balanced agro-industrial communities. Development of

these industries would create employment opportunities for a mass of rural people and in consequence, it will raise their purchasing power. They do not require much skilled manpower. Unskilled labour is easily available by minor training through District Industry Centre. Thus these industries provide an impetus for development[7]. In rural industrialisation, two factors play a significant role, i.e. cheap power and availability of capital. Establishment of thermal power plant at Barauni has helped in industrialisation of Siwan but with the completion of Muzzaffarpur power project and the Gandak product of hydel power, this region can be well placed on the rural industrial map of Bihar. The greatest constraint has been the availability of power, regarding the dispersal of industrial activity. So the generation and transmission of power should gain highest priority in industrial development. It will check the draining away of village resources, and make them sufficient[8].

District Industry Centre : a Better Contribution

District Industry Centre (DIC) has been established in the district in April, 1978. For the first time an institutional framework has been provided to look into the problem of rural industrialisation which earlier was being governed by a single officer known as DIO. This office with its five to eight core functionaries headed by General Manager will bring to each area a capability, both administrative and technical which is basically bringing administration to the people at the grass-roots level[9]. There has been a tremendous increase in the number of industries (100 within a year) after the establishment of DIC but not proportionately increased the employment potential. It is basically an attempt to decentralize industrial administration and will help to set-up new industries based on local raw materials, also in terms of finance and appropriate technology. There are 3 things most important for the successful functioning of the DIC i.e. (1) proposal to set up financial organisation with the help of lead bank— Central Bank of India, (2) establishment of rural marketing centre to provide mechanism for the product, and (3) a production-cum-training workshop is proposed to be established for rural artisans and other skilled workers. Thus, the DIC can emerge as the hub of economic growth in the district. There is also lack of a network of good roads, communication and marketing facilities. With the provision of necessary supporting services and the removal of above deficiencies, it will be possible to develop small industries, which will provide self-employment as well as wage employment and also raise a large number of under privileged sections of the community above the existing poverty line. As long as an organised marketing system for small sector is absent, the large products will have a definite edge over them. The service centre (total 75) strategy to be followed accordingly, so that the exchange system may become more rational.

Notes and References

1 Dande, W.B. 1977, "A Framework of Rural Industrialization", Spl. No. of Invention Intelligence, Vol. 12, Nos. 1 & 2, New Delhi, 61-62.
2. Yapa, L.F., 1977, "Rural Industrialization" in Rural Development Technology, An Integrated Approach, eds. G. Singh and J.H. De Goede, Bangkok : AIT, 367.
3. Roy, P. and Patil, B.R., 1977, Manual for Block Level Planning, New Delhi, The Macmillan, 69.
4. Singh, Rana P.B. and Singh, Ram Babu, 1981, Changing Frontiers of India Village Economy : Case of a Bihari Village-Majhanpura, NGSI Res., Pub. 27, Chap. 8, Varanasi.
5. Molgavkar, P.D. 1971, "Industrialisation of Rural Areas" in Rural Development in Changing Worlds, eds. R. Weitz, The MIT Press, 123.
6. Marsden, K., "The Role of Small Scale Industry in Development Opportunities and Constraints", in New Concepts and Technologies in Third World Urbanisation, ed. Johan Frieadmann, Los Angeles : University of California, S.A., U.P.
7. Weitz, Raanan, 1971, From Peasant to Farmer: A Revolutionary Strategy for Development, New York : Columbia University Press, 130.
8. Behari, B., 1976, Rural Industrialization in India, New Delhi : Vikas, 5-8.
9. Vepa, R.K., 1979, "District Industry Centre : A Leap Forward" in Productivity, January-March, Vol. XIX, No. 4, 545-50.

13

Female Labour Participation in Household and Non-household Industry : India A-Case

ASHOK KUMAR*

Introduction

For centuries woman power has not been mobilised and used for national development and well being by our planners. The 20th century in India or at least the first half of it, is characterised by women's struggle to assert herself as a humanbeing and to gain recognition in the society. Indian society in the last century, and perhaps down the ages, had little regard or use for its girls and women.

Since the beginning of the colonial period, the Indian education was job-oriented i.e. towards producing clerical staff for the East India Company's successor government. The system is our educational heritage and we hug it with reverence in spite of the changes contemplated in our constitution and plans and the recommendations made by successive commissions for reforms. The reason for introducing English medium was to meet the need for clerical staff both in administration and professions. With the attainment of independence, the need for the different orientation became imperative, but hardly any effort has been made to change the structure and pattern of education or relate it to the manpower need of our country.

However, labour is the integral factor of development and its quality as well as quantity affect the specialisation and division of labour and the market for goods and services. The utilization of labour force mainly depends on the supply and demand for labour. The total number of

* Faculty Member at the NIPCCD Regional centre, Lucknow - 226 020 (INDIA)

workers in labour supply is highly affected by the behaviour of the marginal groups particularly women with their dual role of housewife and worker, which not only are changeable but also intermingle in a subsistence economy.

While discussing the participation in production process one has to keep in mind the gender role ideology in the mode of production. One line of thinking is to analyse the development of housewife and their role as a historical product of changes in the economic function of the household and the physical and conceptual separation of domestic work from other kind of work (Gulati, 1975, Oakley, 1976, Srinivas, 1978). From the second point of view women constitute a labour reserve: being defined first and foremost as domestic workers and may be drawn into the industrial work force or excluded from it according to the need of capitalist production (Sinha, 1972, Sharma, 1980). Some micro level studies (Gadgil, 1965, Mitra, 1979, Sharma, 1980, Jain1983, and Kumar, 1989) reveals that women's participation has been declined since 1921. Reasons for the decline of woman's participation in the work-force differ in Urban and Rural areas which are mainly rooted from a strong view that wife's leisure might be taken as a sign of status rather than indigence. The other factors that exhibit women's employment are heavy domestic work load of assumed work, irregular and under payment of wages, absence of transport facilities, lack of child care centres and other supportive structures. It is, however, well documented as well as empirically shown that women are no longer a protected dependent sex in modern India but an active member of this developing nation.

There is no doubt that women and their problems have acquired a steadily growing importance in social research. However, before going into micro level analysis let us have a bird's eye view on sex ratio and female literacy at micro level.

Sex ratio

The sex ratio of the population of India, states and Union Territories are presented in Table 1 and Figs. 1 & 2. The sex ratio in India has been generally adverse to women, i.e. the number of women per 1,000 men has generally been less than 1,000. Apart from being adverse to women, the sex ratio has also declined over the decades. The slight improvement noticed in 1981 Census has not been maintained in 1991 and in fact there has been a fall by five points from 934 in 1981 to 929 in 1991. The reason for the general disparity in the sex ratio and the declining trend over the years need further examination. Studies made so far have offered several explanations for this pheno non in the past. Some of them are : a preference for male children resulting in neglect of female babies, the relative gap in the health conditions between males and females and certain types of mortality which are sex selective. It is also due to lower expectation of life at birth for females in the past compared to males, part of which is due to high maternal mortality.

In the Indian context, a sex ratio of 950 and above can be considered as favourable to females. The states and union territories coming under this category apart from Kerala and Himachal Pradesh are Andhra Pradesh, Goa, Karnataka, Manipur, Orissa, Tamil Nadu, Dadra and Nagar Haveli, Daman and Diu and Pondichery. An analysis of the trends in sex ratio as presented in Fig. 1 indicates that the sex ratio in most of the state has been declined. It has been declining till 1971 but has shown a slight improvement in 1981 and again has declined in 1991. Among the states and union territories, only Kerala has sex ratio favourable to females. The variations in sex ratio in the 12 states which have population of 25 million and above in the 1991 Census are depicted in the Graph (Fig.1) and diagram (Fig.2). The marked variations particularly in Bihar are clearly brought out by the graph. The graph also indicates that certain states have sex ratio close to the all- India ratio of 929. Some of the major states such as Assam, Bihar, Punjab, Rajasthan, Uttar Pradesh and West Bengal have sex ratio below the all-India ratio.

It is evident from the Table 1 that literacy amongst female has gone up from 0.69 per cent in 1901 to 39.42 per cent in 1991. The process, statistically, is no doubt, substantial but still in absolute terms it is far from satisfactory. The female literacy rate by state is presented in (fig. 3) which shows that the states of Andhra Pradesh, Arunachal Pradesh, Bihar, Madhya Pradesh, Meghalaya, Orissa, Rajasthan, Uttar Pradesh and Union Territory of Dadra & Nagar Haveli have literacy rates below the national average. Among different states, Kerala, Mizoram and Goa have maximum literate females. Whereas the minimum literacy rates are noticed in Rajasthan, Bihar, Uttar Pradesh.

Table 1

Process of Literacy Rates in India

Census year	*Percentage of Literates to Total Prop.*			
	Males		*Females*	
	% Increase in a Decade		*% Increase in Decade*	
1901*	9.83	-	0.69	-
1911*	10.56	0.73	1.05	0.36
1921*	12.21	1.65	1.81	0.76
1931*	15.59	3.38	2.93	1.12
1951**	24.95	9.36	7.93	5.00
1961	34.44	9.49	12.95	5.02
1971	39.45	5.01	18.72	5.77
1981@	46.89	7.44	24.82	6.10
1991	63.83	16.87	39.42	14.60

* For undivided India

** Excluded Jammu & Kashmir

© Excluded Assam.

Source: Census of India 1981 & Provisional Table 1991.

After realising the significance role women, an attempt has been made in the present paper to find out the patterns of women's occupational participation in twenty selected states of India. The focus is primarily on the household and non-household industry occupations and investigated with two-digit occupational classifications. It has also been determined that women workers are relegated to low status-ranking occupations and how much scope exists for vertical occupational mobility and identified the major occupations in women worker are in dominance.

Methods of Analysis

For the purpose of present exercise the date have been obtained mainly from 1981 and 1991 censuses. To analyse the role of women in household and non-household industry following methodology has been adopted:

The major groups of industry in India Standard Industrial Classification (ISIC)[1] answering to household[2] and nonhousehold[3], rural and urban are state-wise identified[4]. The idea is to examine specifically the extent of female participation relative to males in household manufacturing sector, which is usually regarded as strong hold of female workers. The index of assessing female participation relative to male is to work out the sex ratio (F/M × 1,000) of participants in each major groups and study the behaviour of this ratio in household and non household activity by major groups urban and rural and different regions. To find out regional differences, it is decided to limit the present exercise to the six political regions of India. The regions are shown in Fig. 4.

For the purpose of analysis of variance, a two-way ANOVA test (with one observation per cell) was applied. The mathematical details are as follows:

Let, *nij* be the value from the *i*-th group and *j*-th region. The linear mathematical model, i.e.

$$nij = \mu + \alpha_i + \beta_i + E_{ij} \tag{1.1}$$

where,

μ is the general mean effect,

α_i is the effect due to *i*-th group,

β_i is the effect due to *j*-th region, and

E_{ij} is the error due to change,

and,

$$\sum_{i=1}^{k} \alpha_i = 0 = \sum_{j=1}^{h} \beta_i \tag{1.2}$$

Null Hypotheses

The null hypothesis is that the groups as well as regions are homogeneous. In other words, the null hypothesis for groups and regions are respectively,

$$\begin{aligned} Hg &: \quad = 2 = \ldots = \quad = 0 \\ Hz &: \beta_1 = \beta_2 = \ldots = \quad = 0 \end{aligned} \tag{1.3}$$

i.e., there is insignificant difference between groups as well as between regions.

$$\text{Now, } St2 = Sg2 + Sz2 = Se\,2 \tag{1.4}$$

where: St2 = is the total sum of squares.

Sg2 = is the S.S. due to Groups.

Sz2 = is the S.S. due to regions.

Se2 = is the S.S. due to Error.

For numerical computation of the various sum of squares the following formulas are used.

Total sum of squares=RSS (Row Sum of Squares)

(T.S.) -c.f. (forrection factor)

$$= \sum_i \sum_j nij - \frac{G^2}{N}$$

$$(\text{C.F.} = \frac{G^2}{N}) \qquad (1.5)$$

Where, G is the grand total of all the cell observation and N = k* h or (rows* columns)

Groups Sum of Squares

$$(\text{GSS}) = \frac{1}{\lambda} \sum_{i=1}^{k} T_j^2 - C.F. \qquad (1.6)$$

Regions Sum of Squares

$$(\text{ZSS}) = \frac{1}{k} \sum_{i=1}^{h} T_j^2 - C.F. \qquad (1.7)$$

Error Sum of Squares is then calculated by subtracting the total of Groups Sum of Squares and Regions Sum of Squares from the Total Sum of Squares.

Table 2

ANOVA Table for Two-way Classified Data

Source of Variation	*Sum of Squares (SS)*	*d.f.*	*M.S.S.*	*Variance Ratio*
1	2	3	4	5
Groups	Sg2 = GSS	$(k-1)$	Sg 2 $(k-1)$	$F_g = \frac{Sg2}{SE2} \sim F\ (k-1), (k-1)\ (h-1)$
Regions	Sz2 = ZSS	$(h-1)$	$\frac{SZ2}{(h-1)}$	$Fz = \frac{Sz\,2}{SE\,2} \sim F\,(h-1)\ (k-1)\,(h-1)$
Error	S2E	$(K-1) \times (h-1)$		$\frac{SE^2}{(k-1)\ (h-1)}$
Total	TSS	$(N-1)$ *or* $(hk-1)$		

The degrees of freedom (d.f.) for Groups, Regions and Error should add up to total d.f.

If the observed value of Fg obtained is greater than the tabulated value of F for $(k-1)$, $(k-1)$ $(h-1)$ d.f. at specified level of significance (usually 5% or 1%) the Hg is refuted as that level otherwise it may be retained. Similarly for Fz. If the Error mean Sum of Squares is less than the M.S.S. of any factor of classification then F is calculated by keeping M.S.S. (Error) in the numerator.

In the ANOVA Table, the values of the variance ratio F which are significant at the given level of significance, has been marked with one asterisk (*). Double asterisk (**) represents highly significant value.

Since variance is independent of change of Origin, the shifting of origin to some arbitrary point, if necessary, also reduces arithmetic to a great extent.

Analysis of Data

It is decided to limit the present exercise to the six political regions of India to find out whether significant regional differences exist. Besides, analysis on the basis of all the States and Union Territories would be a very large undertaking. The analysis has been thus confined to variations in the sex ratio participation in rural and urban areas of each of the six industrial classification of household and non-household industry.

Ranking of Regions

The first three Major Groups (MG) in order of total number of workers employed in different regions are given in Table 3. It is evident from the table that in 4 Regions Major Group-27 (i.e. Manufacture of Wood and Wood products, furniture and fixture) occupies first order followed by Major Group 26 (i.e. Manufacture of Textile Products, other than Footwear).

Non-household industry classification runs through all the 9 Divisions of the Industrial Classification. Among the different Divisions, the Divisions 2 and 3 (Manufacturing and Repair) occupies the first position followed by, Division 9 (Community, Social and Personal Services) and Division 6 (Wholesale and Retail Trade Hotels). The highest ranking is occupied by Division 2 and 3 for all the regions, followed by Division 9 and 6, although not always in that order in every region.

Ranking of Sex-Ratio of Workers

The sex ratio of workers (i.e. 1000 × Female/Male) other than in cultivation was computed for all industrial major groups. In the ideal circumstances of men and women participating equally in every industry or activity, this ratio would be 1000. However, the sex ratio for rural/urban household and non-household industry has been calculated for all, the Major Groups are rearranged according to sex ratio category. The consolidated Table 4 gives frequency of each of the sex ratio categories. The percentage frequency columns convert the absolute frequencies in the frequency columns into percentages, categories I to VI together being taken as 100. The cumulating percentage frequency (to identify the greater-than-type groups) column adds up the percentage frequencies from bottom upwards to the figure 100 in each case.

For household industry India as a whole, 80 per cent (85% for rural and 80% for urban) of the Major Groups fall in the low flrequency category IV (250-499). While in non-household industry this percentage is more than 90 per cent. In other words, proportion of women employed is less than half of men in more than two-third of the Major Groups. This does not bring out the gravity of the situation quite fully. In fact, in one-fifth (20 per cent in rural and 25 per cent in urban) the proportion of women employed is in the very low grading, being as little as between twentieth and a quarter of men employed.

The corresponding picture in non-household industry is much more disturbing, in fact alarming. The maximum participation frequency (34 rural and 36 urban) occurs in the low category V (50 to 249) and 42 per cent of rural and 44 per cent of urban of the Major Groups fall in category VI (Lowest). This means that only in one per cent of the Major Groups in rural non-household industry does the participation of women exceed half of that of men. The great bulk of the rural non-household industry Major Groups have a participation rate of women which varies between a twentieth and a quarter (50-250) of that of men.

As reflected by the sex ratio figures for household and non-household industry, the position of female workers in both rural and urban areas is quite alarming, indeed precarious. Generally speaking, more than 85 per cent of the Major Groups in household and non-household industry, rural and urban, have sex ratios falling in category IV and below. In other words, not more than 15 per cent of the Major Groups have sex ratios which can be called High, Moderate or Low Moderate, with female participation rates of 500 and above.

Analysis of Results

An examination of the results in Table 5 (analysis of variance dealing with rural household industry workers) shows that there is no significant variation in the number of females per 1000 males between regions. But the variation in sex ratio among Major Groups is significant at 1 per cent level. Statistically speaking, the mean sex ratios for six regions are not quite different from each other. On the other hand, all Major Groups do not have equal mean sex ratio. This inequality of mean sex ratio for all Major Groups having been established, the next obvious question will be to identify the major Group that has the highest mean sex ratio.

However, Table 6 shows the results of analysis of variance for urban household industry work. The results are significant at 1 per cent level, meaning thereby significant variations exist in both Groups as well as regions. Hence, we have not calculated the critical differences for this particular Table, whereas for other three tables ranking and critical differences have been worked out. The task thereafter will be to rank all other Major Groups by the decreasing mean sex ratio. This is what is done in the first three columns of Table 9, with the first column containing the description of the Major Groups of the highest six and the lowest six mean sex ratios.

After ranking the Major Groups, one would like to know whether one Major Groups was statistically different from another, that is, to go in for pair-wise comparisons in terms of mean sex ratio. The comparison of one Major Group with another next in rank is done by comparing the mutual mean difference given in the fourth column of Table 9 with the computer critical differences given at the bottom of the table.

The differences in the ranking of regions in rural household industry is presented in the first left hand column in Table 9. This shows the significant differences between regions: the north-eastern commands the highest mean sex ratio follows by southern, eastern, northern. Central and Western respectively. The means sex ratio for north-eastern region is significantly different from that of southern.

Tables 7 and 8 show that the variance among regions as well as among major Groups is not significant at 1 per cent level. The ranking of regions presented in the Table 9 puts the southern (in rural non-household industry) north-eastern (in urban non-household industry) at the top. The ranking of regions in terms of mean sex ratio, with the qualifying observation that the mean sex ratio for each of them is very low.

Since regions show significant differences, instead of calculating students (t) for different pairs of regions, we calculated the least significant difference at the given level of significance. This least difference is known as the critical difference (CD) and calculated by the formula given below:

$$\sqrt{\frac{2\ Se^2}{r}} \times t\ 0.05 \text{ for error d.f.} \qquad (1.8)$$

where,

Se^2 = Mean Sum of Square (M.S.S.)

r = Regions i.e. 6

We arrange the region's mean in their descending order of magnitude. However, the results are presented in the Tables. We therefore, conclude that the difference between mean of north-eastern region and southern regions are significantly different from each other since the difference between their mean, viz., 1437 exceeds critical difference i.e., 313.49. All the remaining differences are not significant.

Findings

The discussion in this paper is proof of the limited number of industries in which women participate to any significant degree. Activities engaging higher rates of female participation in household industry are industries relating to different textiles, tobacco products or forestry and logging which are characterised by high labour intensity and tediousness, less mobility, less skill, coupled with less remuneration. On the other hand, some of the Major Groups in non-household industry are commanding higher rates of female participation. This marked difference in work participation for women in many Major Groups in household industry several in non-household industry, where higher female participation is invariably characterised by heavy manual labour, drudgery, insanitary conditions of work, and low remuneration, may very possibly have undesirable impacts on society through first, high mortality rate of women (continuous decline in sex ratio in the population since 1901 is disturbing, to say the least) and, second, through the motivation of increasing the family second, through, motevation of increamy family size to lessen the burden of economic struggle.

NOTES

1. Report of the the Committee on the Status of Women in India, *Towards Equality,* Govt. of India, Deptt. of Social Welfare, Ministry of Education, p. 148.
2. Kumar A. (1989) : *Indian Women Towards 21st Century,* Criterion Publications, New Delhi, p. 8.
3. **Ibid**. p.8.
4. The study is based on the 1981 industrial classification. The Indian Standard Classification (ISC) classifies the industrial distribution of workers into 9 divisions and 99 Major Groups.
5. Household industry is strictly limited to manufacturing on the household level and excluded manufacturing outside house.
6. Non-household industry, spous manufacturing, construction, trade and commerce, transport, communication and service.
7. Household industry in the Census of India, 1981 is confined to Division 2 and 3 only and the major and minor groups comprising them.

REFERENCES

Gadgil, D.R. (1965), *Women in the Working Force in India,* Asia Publishing House, Delhi.

Gulati, Leela (1975), 'Inter-State Difference in Female Labour Force Participation', *Economic and Political Weekly,* Vol. 10, Nos. 1-2, January 11.

Jain, Devaki (1984), Displacement of Women in Traditional Industries, ISST.

Kumar, Ashok (1989), *Indian Women Towards 21st Century,* Criterion Publications, New Delhi.

Mitra, Asok (1978), 'Employment of Women', *Manpower,* 14 (1), April-June, New Delhi.

Oaklyley, A. (1974), *Housewife,* Penguin, London.

Sharma, Ursula (1980), Women Work and Property in North West India,, Tavistock Publishing House, London.

Sinha, J.N. (1975), 'Female Work Participation': A Comment', Economic and Political Weekly, 10(16), April 19.

Srinivas, M.N. (1978), *The Changing Position of Indian Women,* Oxford University Press, Bombay, India.

Table 3

A–First–three Major Groups Employed in Household Industry in Different Regions

Region	*First order groups*	*Second order groups*	*Third order groups*
1	*2*	*3*	*4*
India	Mg–23 (Manufacture of cotton textiles)	MG–27 (Manufacture wood and wood products, furniture and fixtures)	MG–39 (Repair)
Northern	MG–26 (Manufacture of Textile Products) (other than Footwear)	MG–27 (Manufacture of wood and wood products, furniture and fixtures)	MG–39 (Repair)
Central	MG–26 (Manufacture of textile products (other than footwear)	MG–39 (Repair)	MG–27 (Manufacture of wood and wood products, furniture and fixture).
Eastern	MG–27 (Manufacture of wood and wood products, furniture and fixtures)	MG–23 (Manufacture of cotton Textiles)	MG–32 (Manufacture of Non-Metallic Mineral products)
North-Eastern	MG–27 (Manufacture of wood and wood products, furniture and fixtures)	MG–39 (Repair)	MG–23 (Manufacture of cotton textiles)
Western	MG–27 (Manufacture of wood and wood products, furniture and fixture)	MG–39 (Repair)	MG–26 (Manufacture of Textile Products (other than Footwear)
Southern	MG–27 (Manufacture of wood and wood products, furniture and fixtures)	MG–39 (Repair)	MG–26 (Manufacture of Textile Products (other than Footwear)

Table 3

B–First–three Major Groups in Non-Household Industry in Different Regions

Region	*First order groups*	*Second order groups*	*Third order groups*
1	*2*	*3*	*4*
India	MG–65 (Retail Trade in Food and Articles, Beverages, Tobacco and Intoxicants)	MG–70 (Land Transport)	MG–90 (Public Admn. and Defence Services)
Northern	MG–70 (Land Transport)	MG–65 (Retail Trade in Food Article, Beverages, Tobacco and Intoxicants)	MG–02 (Live stock Production)
Central	MG–65 (Retail Trade in Food and Food Articles, Beverages, Tobacco and intoxicants)	MG–70 (Land Transport)	MG–99 (Services not elsewhere where classified)
Eastern	MG–65 (Retail Trade in Food and Food Articles, Beverages, Tobacco and Intoxicants)	MG–90 (Public Admn. and Defence services)	MG–70 (Land Transport)
North-Eastern	MG–90 (Public Admn. and Defence Services)	MG–65 Retail Trade in Food and Food Articles, Beverages, Tobacco and intoxicants)	MG–70 (Land Transport)
Western	MG–70 (Land Transport)	MG–90 (Public Admn. and Defence services)	MG–65 (Retail Trade in Food and Food Articles Beverages, Tobacco and intoxicants)
Southern	MG–65 (Retail Trade in Food and Food Articles Beverages, Tobacco and intoxicants)	MG–70 (Land Transport)	MG–90 (Public Admn. and Defence Services)

Table 4

Percentage Frequency of Participation Sex Ratio in India – Six Regions by Rural and Urban Household and Non–Household Industry, 1987 (Sex Ratio Categorisation : I. Over 1000, II 750–999, III. 500–749 IV. 250–249, VI. Below 50)

Category	*Freque-ncy*	*Percent-age Freque ncy*	*Cumulative Percentage Frequency*	*Frequency*	*Percentage Frequency*	*Cumulative Percent Frequency*
1	*2*	*3*	*4*	*5*	*6*	*7*
Household Industry India						
I	1	5	100	3	15	100
II	1	5	95	0	0	85
III	1	5	90	1	5	85
IV	8	40	85	3	15	80
V	5	25	45	8	40	65
VI	4	20	20	5	25	25
Total	20	100		20	100	
Non-Household Industry India						
1	*2*	*3*	*4*	*5*	*6*	*7*
I	0	0	100	0	0	100
II	1	1	100	0	0	100
III	0	0	99	2	3	100
IV	7	10	99	2	3	97
V	34	47	89	36	50	94
VI	31	42	42	31	44	44
Total	73	100		73	100	

Table 5

Analysis of Variance for Rural Household Industry Workers, 1981

Source	*Degree of Freedom (DF)*	*Sum of Squares (SS)*	*Mean Sum of Squares (MSS)*	*F–value*
Major Group	18	38974794	2165266	28.213**
Region	5	37160228	7432045	96.83**
Error	90	6907223	76747	
Total	113	83042245	—	—

Note: Double Asterisk indicates insignificant at 1% level.

Table 6

Analysis of Variance for Urban Household Industry Workers, 1981

Source value	*Degree of Freedom (DF)*	*Sum of Squares (SS)*	*Mean Sum of Squares (MSS)*	*F–value*
Major Group	18	466397038	25910947	1.074*
Region	5	0159224271	31844854	1.32*
Error	90	2171957121	24132857	—
Total	113	2797578430	—	—

Note: Single Asterisk indicates significant at 1% level.

Table 7

Analysis of Variance for Rural Non-household Industry Workers, 1981

Source	*Degree of Freedom (DF)*	*Sum of Squares (SS) SE^2*	*Mean Sum of Squares (MSS) SE^2*	*F–value*
Major Group	63	5747390	89802	4.79**
Region	5	565605	113121	6.04**
Error	320	7305441	18731	—
Total	389	13618436	—	—

Note: Double Asterisk indicates insignificant at 1% level.

Table 8

Analysis of Variance for Urban Non-household Industry Workers, 1981

Source	*Degree of Freedom (DF)*	*Sum of Squares (SS)*	*Mean Sum of Squares (MSS)*	*F–value*
Major Group	63	7561988	120031	2.65**
Region	5	1212066	242413	5.34**
Error	315	14290799	45367	—
Total	383	23064853	—	—

Note: Double Asterisk indicates insignificant at 1% level.

Table 9

Ranking of Regions
Rural Household Industry

Region	*Mean*	*Mutual Mean Difference*
North-Eastern	1778	1437
Southern	341	84
Eastern	257	23
Northern	234	4
Central	230	39
Western	191	—

Critical Difference (5% Level) = 313.49

Rural Non-Household Industry

Region	*Mean*	*Mututal Mean Difference*
Southern	178	6
North-Eastern	172	24
Western	148	22
Central	126	19
Eastern	107	39
Northern	68	—

Urbab Non-Household Industry

Region	*Mean*	*Mututal Mean Difference*
North-Eastern	231	77
Southern	154	31
Western	123	45
Northern	78	1
Eastern	77	2
Central	75	—

Critical Difference (5% Level) = 241.02

14

Women's Participation in Rural Local Level Institution

DR. MUKTA MITTAL

Introduction

In India determining the status of women factors such as the role of women in decision-making in the family and in the community. Their educational status, their participation in social, political and economic activities and their position in various professions as well as their legal status in terms of marriage, divorce and inheritance of property should be taken into consideration. Although distributive justice has been categorically underlined in all the development plan, the needs of women have not been adequately addressed. However, a majority of women in rural areas attend to domestic work (43.8 million in the age group of 15-49 years) and those who are engaged in free collection of goods (vegetables, roots, fish, firewood, cattle feed, etc.) and providing services (sewing, weaving, maintenance of kitchen garden, orchards, poultry etc.) (26.6 million). Although rural women constitute a large section of population of the country. Their lives are still characterised by hand work drudgery and without any basic amenities. They are trapped in the vicious circle of low income, ill-health, low nutrition, low productivity, and low wages. As a result women are considered as target groups in the community development programme (1952).

The programme envisaged under community development had a strong component for womens development social education, etc. Recognising the importance of democratic institution at grass-root level. The Panchayati (village council) at village level was established in1961. The Panchayat Raj institutions were in fact considered to be the most effective instruments for realising the goals of economic betterment and social justice for the least privileged. Participation of women, who constitute nearly half of the population, in Panchayati Raj institution has been considered ensential for enabling them to participate effectively and independently in democratic and political processes and to influence decision-making. It has been recognised as a step towards equal society and a means of realising the development goals for women.

Legislations Related To Women's Involvement in Panchayat

The first voice on a national level for a Constitutional amendment was heard in 1978 with the Ashok Mehta Committee report which had even appended a Draft Constitution Amendment Bill to make Panchayats "an organic integral part of our democratic process". The argument for it gained momentum in the second half of the Eighties. There were two reasons for it. First, the concentration of power in Delhi had reached a flash point threatening to break the very foundations of our polity. Therefore, "power to the people" became a slogan which demanded decentralised structures down at the village level. Second, the popularity of the Governments which had implemented successful panchayats in West Bengal and Karnataka had sent signals that this was an effective instrument to win the hearts of the rural masses. The concrete measures taken in 1989 to give constitutional sanction for panchayats has now borne fruit after about four years of tortuous journey.

The 64th Amendment Bill passed by the Lok Sabha but defeated in the Rajya Sabha in October 1989 as well as the 74th Amendment Bill introduced in Parliament in September 1990 by the National Front Government have been discussed threadbare. The present Bill when it was introduced in 1991 as well as the report of the Joint Committee of Parliament as this Bill had attracted wide-spread attention. However, some aspects of the Bill as passed on December 22 and 23, 1992 by the Lok Sabha and the Rajya Sabha respectively require our critical appraisal.

The major flaw of the Bill is that it has adopted a uniform three-tier system below the State level. Even in bigger states like Karnataka, Tamil Nadu and Assam which had three-tiers, there were structural differences. Haryana, Manipur, Kerala and Sikkim and the Union Territory of Lakshadweep had only two-tiers. Goa, Jammu and Kashmir, Tripura and several Union Territories had only one-tier. It would have been better to leave the States to decide the number of tiers, given their specific socio-historical milieu. It looks artificial to create a fixed number of tiers irrespective of their history and tradition. The

AIADMK and the DMK members spoke vehemently against this three-tier uniformity from their experience of Tamil Nadu but theirs was a lone voice. Even the Marxist dissenting voice which spoke against uniformity in legislation finally gave in. The only concession given is that at the intermediate level. The panchayats may not be constituted in States which have less than 20 Lakh population.

Wherever the panchayats have not taken roots or have been uprooted after brief spells of success, it has been observed that Members of Parliament and State legislatures have not been too friendly to these institutions. Not only have they been indifferent to local governments. But also hostile to there bodies, at times. No one would like to see another centre of power emerging as a challenge, nor would they like to see their existing powers being diluted. So much so, one feels that had it not been for the fact that the State legislatures were created along with Parliament, our respected MPs would not have allowed even the State legislatures to come up after a few years of tasting power.

The Constitutional status accorded to the panchayats, which was a whipping boy of the bureaucrats, MLAs, MPs, and both rural urban elite, well be a success story only with a strong peoples movement to give it the necessary momentum.

So for as women's involvement and participation in Panchayati Raj institution is concern, it is marginal. Considering this the policy- makers since very beginning had kept some provision for women's participation in the Panchayati Raj. Initially as many as 30 per cent reservation was there for women which has been increased up to 40 per cent recently. Even then their participation in the panchayati raj institutions have not yet increased.

73rd Amendments

The 73rd amendment of the Constitution is a revolutionary step towards establishment of grass-root democracy in the country. This amendment, to be precise, implies the following major changes in the area of development administration:

(i) Panchayat election has become mandatory and it has to be held at the interval of every five years as in the case of the State Assembly and the Parliament. Even if the elected body is superseded election has to be held within six months of the supersession.

(ii) 33% of the elected members of the Panchayat have to be women condidates.

(iii) Reservation of seats for scheduled castes and tribes has also been ensured based on the percentage of population of these groups of people.

(iv) The Panchayats will have much bigger responsibilities in raising resources locally.

(v) The Panchayats will have power to prepare its own plan for which the Government financial support will be available. In case of Jawahar Rozgar Yojana 80% of such funds will go directly to the village Panchayat. 50% of the district planned budget will go to the Zilla Parishad and the Parishad will divert the fund to the Panchayat Samitis based on their action plans.

Participation of Women in Panchayati Raj Institutions

The introduction of democratic Decentralisations resulted in the establishment of Panchayat. But in most of the Panchayati Raj legislations enacted by different state Government women were to be co-opted under special category. This did not result into the development of village leadership among women and their participation in the decision-making process. In this connection the Committee on the status of women in the Panchayati Raj Institutions has not been effective either in articulating women's needs, or in mobilising women for adequate participation. Taking note of this fact the Committee on Panchayati Raj Institutions recommended: (a) increasing representation of women in these institutions; (b) establishing a special committee of women Panchayat members and power and funds to ensure that the decisions are made by women themselves on priorities and choice in welfare and development programmes specifically for women and children; (c) provision of institutional finance and budget support for rural industrialisation projects for women; and (d) strengthening the constructive decision-making and managerial roles; (e) Mahila-mandals to ensure full access to development resources and services.

The data regarding women's participation in Panchayati Raj Bodies (1979-80) for all India are presented in the following Table.

Table 1

Women's Participation in Panchayati Raj Bodies 1979–80 (— All India)

Sl. No.	*Items*	*Numbers*
1.	Women Members of Gram Panchayats	
	(a) Elected	41,207
	(b) Coopted	1,00,385
	(c) Total	1,41,592
2.	Women Members of Panchayat Samitis	
	(a) Elected	595
	(b) Coopted	1,136
	(c) Total	1,731
3.	No. of womens Sarpanches	506

Source: Rural Development Statistics, NIRD, Hyderabad, 1982

Table 2

Extent of Womens Participation in Panchayati Raj Bodies

Sl. No.	*Items*	*Numbers*
1.	Percentage of elected women members of Gram Panchayat	19.41 (29.10)
2.	Percentage of coopted women members of Gram Panchayat to total number of Gram Panchayat	47.29 (70.90)
3.	Percentage of elected women members of Panchayat Samitis to total No. of Panchayat Samitis	13.27
4.	Percentage of coopted women members of Panchayat Samitis to total number of Panchayat Samitis	25.35
5.	Percentage of women Sarpanches to total number of Gram Panchayats	0.23

Note: Percentage of total, elected plus coopted

Source: as for Table 1.

It is clear from the above table that participation of women in Panchayati Raj Institutions were very marginal. Out of 2,12,248 Gram Panchayats only 506 (0.23 per cent) women Sarpanches were elected. The number of elected women members were very few (19.10 per cent) in both the cases, Gram Panchayats as well as Panchayat Samitis. Further, if we have a look at the elected women members of Gram

Panchayat to total number of panchayats, it was only about one fifth (19.41 per cent). Again, in the Panchayat Samitis a little more than one-fourth (25-35 per cent), women members were coopted and only 13.27 per cent were elected.

However, the above statistics exhibit that women's participation in the Panchayati Raj is not up to the mark. It is felt that more reservations will not solve the problem unless womens members are given commensurate powers to function effectively. Panchayats should be given real autonomy and not subjected to excessive governmental controls. And then only women members of Panchayats will welcome the concept of Nayaya Panchayats.

Leadership Role

The establishment of the Institution of Village Council (Panchayat) at village level in 1961 also provided opportunities to women to participate in the decision-making process. Women participation in these bodies was encouraged by coopting them as a special category. Women's participation in village based institutions proved to be the most effective instrument in bringing about a change in their way of life in terms of economic well being and adoption of new technology.

Participation of women in the village based on formal and non-formal organisations has been, made significant changes in their social status as well as their position within the family. Further, more participation of women in these organisation is a clear indication of a change in the traditional norms which restricted free movements of a female member in society for social and political activities; women were executed to participate in such economic, and social activites which were confined to the domestic spheres. Any deviation from this norm naturally resulted in an improvement in her position in the society. Participation of women in different organisations thus have two important connotations (i) it gives them a status in the society, and (ii) it permits contribution of women not only in rural development process but also for their own development. It also gives them an opportunity to (a) work in groups on project of common interest; (b) associate with the on-going development programmes; (c) participate in the decision-making, process; (d) articulate women's needs; (e) leadership in the national development process.

The emerging women leadership in rural areas is to a large extent characterised by middle age, high literacy rate and income. However, in the light of the socio-economic features of the village leadership it will be found that the characteristic features of women leadership in rural India are at variance in terms of age, education and occupation. As a result, the rural womens have, in the first instance, been able to identify themselves as an important segment in the society. It has also helped in attracting the attention of the official functionaries to design and implement programmes for the benefit of women. This is evident from the fact that a number of specific programmes specifically meant for women beneficiaries in the field of education, health, employment, family welfare, vocational training have been designed and implemented in recent years.

As a result, rural women have also started showing considerable interest in organising joint economic ventures such as thrift societis, dairy cooperatives, poultry and cattle farming, agricultural and allied activities, weaving and so on. The nature of these groups vary from place to place depending upon their pattern of work and availability of technical and financial assistance from outside. The change from home based action which has prevailed all along to collective action has made a significant change in the life style of people.

Conclusion

The introduction of women's organisation and the consequant emergence of women leadership at the grass-roots level has brought about social changes in the rural women's life, in particular and village communities in general. These organisations have the necessary potential for bringing about more changes rapidly and if given proper opportunity and assistance these can provide further strides in the development of rural women.

The National perspective plan (1988-2000 A.D.) suggested the need for proper training for all women members of panchayats and other bodies to enable them to exercise their authority adequately.

The formal reservation of women in Panchayati Raj Structures through reservation of seats, election, etc. is not a sufficient condition for their effective participation unless and until it is supplemented by measures which help in resolving the socio-economic pressures inhibiting them. The same can be realised by mobilising women through awareness compaign and inter-personal communication by implementing the scheme which help them in attaining economic independance and by enhancing educational facilities at their door steps.

It will be wrong to think that Panchayati Raj should be viewed as a God that has failed. It has many achievements to its credit, the more important of which may be identified here. Politically its inception has become democratic seed-drilling in the Indian society, making an average citizen more conscious of his rights than before. Administratively, it bridged the gulf between the bureaucratic elite and the people socially, it generated a new leadership which was young having a modern and pre-social outlook. Finally, viewed from the developmental angle, it helped rural people to cultivate a developmental angle.

As far as women's participation in the Panchayati Raj is concerned. It is not up to the mark. It is observed that more reservation will not solve the problem unless women members are given commensurate powers to function effectivly. However in this regard the following steps have been suggested:

1. all women members of panchayats and other executive bodies must be trained and empowered to exercise their authority;
2. particular attention must be paid to the development of interpersonal communication skills among the trainees/community leaders;
3. efforts are required to elicit participation of women through establishing links between the elected representatives and the development functionaries;
4. programmes meant for women's development should be linked with panchayat/local functionaries for more effective participation of women;
5. despite being members of these democratic bodies or even their head, women's political participation may be severely constrained by various socio-economic pressures. It would, therefore, be necessary to supplement formal representation in institutional structures with other measures such as mobilisation of women and involvement of panchayats on specific socio-economic issues; and
6. there is need to organise women workers either in a cooperative or any other form whereby production and marketing are integrated. Government institutions or voluntary welfare organisations must come forward to organise women who are self-employed and reduce their exploitation and active participations in panchayats.

Acknowledgement

The author gratefully acknowledge the generous support of Dr. Sunit Gupta while completion of the paper.

References

1. Kumar, Ashok (1993): Women's Participation in Local Bodies in edit book *Women in Contemporary India Society*, Anmol Publication, New Delhi.
2. Mathew George (1993) : From Legislation to a Movement, published in the daily Newspaper *'THE HINDU', Saturday, January 9.*
3. Chakraborty, S.S. (1993) : 73rd Amendment of the Constitution and the Role of the Valuntary Organisations unpublished paper presented in National Worship on Local Self Governance: Role of Voluntary Organisations (August 27-28), organised by VANI, New Delhi.
4. Kumar Ashok (1993) : **Op. Cit.**

15

Rural Development has Miles To Go

SUNIT GUPTA & MUKTA MITTAL

That the real India lives in the villages is an old heard it at some point of time. Yet few of us know that the real India we talk about consists of 33.4 per cent of the rural population living below the poverty line. Progressive industrialization, modernity, and development all of which characterize the new India seem to have left three-fourths of the nation's population untouched in the villages.

Still caught in the mire of uneducation, backwardness and poverty, rural India stands in stark contrast to its glamourous urban counterpart today. Efforts have been on, especially through the consecutive Five Year Plans to bring rural development at par with runaway urbanization. After four decades of planning and implementation the exercise has not achieved the desired results.

Land reforms can be called the engine of socio-economic transformation and rural development. From a feudalistic pattern of land distribution, characteristic of the Raj land reforms have moved towards more socialistic schemes after independence. The Acts were included in the Ninth Schedule of the Constitution so that these could not be challenged in the Courts of Law. In their five-fold scope, land reforms include abolition of intermediaries which have been attempted through suitable enactment since 1984.

Secondly, ceilings were imposed on land holdings to specify the maximum limit land could be held. Agrarian reorganization like preventing fragmentation and ensuring consolidation of holdings was initiated, but in all these areas the necessary determination has been lacking to effectively undertake action. The Sixth Plan (1980-85) document categorically states that the unsatisfactory progress in land reforms "has not been due to flaws in policy but due to indifferent implementation".

Organization of co-operative farms and tenancy reforms like regulation of rent, security of tenure and transfer of ownership to cultivators have enjoyed sporadic successes around the country. For example, in West Bengal, Operation Barga which recognizes the rights of the cultivator to have enjoyed sporadic successes around the country. For example, in West Bengal, Operation Barga which recognizes the rights of the cultivator to the land and ensures against his forcible eviction has had a significant productivity and welfare impact. The fact is land reforms constitute a vital element both in terms of the anti-poverty strategy and for modernization and increased productivity in agriculture. Redistribution of land provides a permanent asset base to the rural landless poor.

Panchayati Raj

West Bengal's concept of decentralization through panchayats to bring about rational development has earned praise even from Lewis Preston, the president of the World Bank. West Bengal's panchayats are by far the most developed in the country, their success attributed to open participation of political parties in the elections. Beginning 1978, West Bengal has regularily held elections every five years. The fourth in the series held on May 29,1993. In most other states, panchayat elections are not held in time. The three states that followed West Bengal's lead with their own versions of political panchayats, viz. Karnataka, Andhra Pradesh and Kerala, the experiments did not survive changes of government at the state level.

Now with the introduction of the 73rd Constitutional Amendment Act 1992, a definite step has been taken towards establishing the Panchayati Raj Institution (PRI) throughout the country. It not only give representation to the Members of Parliament (MPs), MLAs and Members of the Legislative Council (MLCs) at the intermediate and district level PRIs with full voting rights, but also ensures direct elections to all the panchayat seats after a tenure of five years.

The Bill also ensures reservation of seats for SC and ST and more remarkably one-third of the total seats are earmarked for women. How far this move will be successful, in the midst of poor literacy levels and discrimination on casteist and sexist lines, remains as big a problem as ever.

Employment

The constitution of Gram Sabhas in villages and the three-tier panchayats at the viallage and other levels is a welcome step since participation of the people and their representatives will significantly help in implementation of the Jawahar Rozgar Yojana (JRY) which has been put under the direct charge of the PRIs. The JRY merges two wage employment programmes, viz., the National Rural Employment Programme and the Rural Landless Employment Guarantee Scheme into a single programme. The JRY targets the 33.4 per cent of the rural population below the poverty line as the main beneficiaries with preference accorded to women and the SCs. and STs.

The center-piece of the government's employment generation effort for JRY is to be refurnished for the financial year 1993-94. The Rs. 3,300 crore scheme is to be split into two major parts. About Rs. 2,000 crore would continue to fund the scheme as it exists now; the remainder of the money would go towards now; the remainder of the money would go towards additional funding of 100 or so specially selected districts so as to augment employment opportunities in these more backward areas. Besides investing large funds in the more needy regions, the Scheme would also be finetuned to make it more effective on the ground.

Thus, for rigid adherence to the 60:40 norm (60 per cent of the funds were to spent as wages and only 40 per cent towards cost of material) meant the creation of poor quality assets. As a result, the scheme remained a measure of providing only temporary employment with little or no long-term employment created out of the money invested in the scheme. Greater encouragement will now be given for networking i.e. dovetailing the scheme with other developmental activities in the gram panchayat area. Net working would allow finances required for the purchase of material to be provided as a past of other Schemes. The wage component would be paid at of JRY funds. For instance, if a school building was required, money for the construction material could be made available through Operation Blackboard whereas the labour component could come from the JRY. Through this 'networking' was allowed earlier, this is to be given a major thrust.

The greatly enhanced outlay for JRY (upto Rs. 3,306 crore for Financial year 1993-94 from the Rs. 2,546 crore in 1992-93 has meant that the division in to two parts will become possible. Planning Commission officials had been working on this proposal much before the budget, so it is nuclear how they expected the scheme to take root without the additional funds. If the level of funding did not change much, concentration of specific districts would mean diminished funding for the other regions.

Critics, however, argue that all this is mere window dressing. They believe that much of the JRY funds in the past have been wasted and fear that the additional outlay will only increase leakages. The biggest criticism is that the delivery mechanism has not been examined critically and as a result much of the money will continue to be skimmed off by corrupt officials. For instance, only about 57 per cent of the money is left to the panchayats to spend. As the remainder is decided at the level of the block DRDA, accountability and prioritization of village requirements becomes a casualty in many instances. Also the lack of a duly-elected Pancahyat System means that government nominees and their cronies continue to central large sums of money years after year.

Yet, problems affecting rural development are manifold. Thus, success in one sector is immediately offset by drawbacks in others. For instance, a creditable achievement has been the lowering of the poverty level in rural India from a whopping in rural India from a whopping 51.2 per cent of the population to 33.4 per cent in the period 1977-78. But alongside, the rural population has witnessed a decadel growth of nearly 24 per cent in about the same period, i.e. 1981-91.

Problems, some of which have plagued the nation for centuries, coupled with lackluster progress in rural development have left the larger part of the country still in a primitive state. Some problems still remain largely unsorted. Problems of this population growth, increased rural impoverishment, unemployment, differential priorities accorded to urban and rural industrial growth, and low levels of access to social services and linkages like education, health and communication, marginalisation of women and under privileged classes and an alarming deteriorations in quality of physical environment are yet to be addressed on a war-footing.

Lightning up this gloom are rays of hope in the guise of various programmes and schemes in various stages of planning and implementation. The Integrated Rural Development Programme (IRDP) launched in 1978-79 is one such pat-breaking plan. It was designed to effectively tackle rural poverty and create gainful employment and assets for the downtrodden in rural areas. The District Rural Development Agencies (DRDAs) were set up for this purpose.

Two sub-scheme of IRDP and Children in Rural Area Youth for Self-employment (TRYSEM). Experience shows specific target for coverage of women beneficiaries, its flow of assistance to women was marginal and did not wholly serve its purpose. There are innumerable classes where a women member of the family is totally unaware of the loan that has been granted in her name with the male members of the family deciding the mode of utilization of the funds. The specially designed DWCRA was launched in 1982-83 with special assistance of the UNICEF to focus sharply on rural women and adopt pragmatic approach for offering the service of the IRDP to women.

TRYSEM, launched on August 19,1979 concentrates on equipping rural youth in the age-group 18-35 years with necessary skills and technology to take up vocations of self-employment in agriculture and allied activities, industry, services and business. On completion of training, the TRYSEM beneficiaries are assisted under the IRDP.

"Project 2000'' a brainchild of the National Foundation of India's United Kingdom Chapter, has been launched in New Delhi to help the Under Privileged in India.

The chapter would be adopting its first project in Madhya Pradesh cluster of villages covering a 10 km area with the aim of undertaking their social and economic uplift. The interactive aid strategy being geared to the year 2000 and beyond. The aim of the voluntary organization was to channel the energies, resources and professional expertise of India and other UK citizen into contributing towards the building of a happy and prosperous rural India.

It was also planned to adopt a cluster of villages in each of India's States and Union Territories by the beginning of the 21st century. The development of villages would become catalysts for regional development on the same pattern as Indian Green Revolution.

During the first phase from 1993 to 1995, besides the adoption of a cluster of villages in MP and an agriculture college nearby, it is proposed to prepare an integrated development project for the villages with aim that within five years the average household income should reach the national average. The area to produce three crops a year on 80 per cent of the land, basic literacy to be 100 per cent (child and adult schools) and the birth rate to drop below 1 per cent moreover, the 10 km radius of the adopted area would boost its own road, sanitation, piped water, electricity and a monsoon fed lake for fishing and recreation purposes. The

Project office would operate profitably its civic services such as sanitation, piped water and electricity on a commercial basis. Also, as commercial wing would operate demonstration farms, seed supply store, grain store, village cooperative super market, irrigation pumps, tractors and implements and cold storage for perishable goods and milk and butter dairy.

Banking

To encourage domestic savings by rural women, the government launched a scheme by which a village woman who managed to start a bank account with minimum of Rs. 300 a year, will earn a government contribution of Rs 75 to her account. The government has earmarked. Rs. 10,000 crore for this purpose. The latest scheme of Mahila Samriddhi Yojana (MSY) is the link in the chain of special programmes taken up in the planned rural development process. The scheme covers the wide base of 70 per cent of total women population living in villages. The objective is simple to sensitize women about their rule in economic activities and cultivate the habit of saving. The target is to cover 6 crore adult females by the end of the Eighth Plan. One crore accounts are expected to be opened in the first year. In the very first month, more than 1.15 lakh accounts with a deposit of more than one crore have been opened in 19 states and Union Territories across the country. Sensitizing women at the grass-roots in the rural areas through MSY falls in line with "All round development" objective envisaged in the National Perspective Plan for Women (1988-2000). MSY is also significant in the context of integrated development of rural areas as 30 per cent of households are headed by women.

Housing

Financial support is also extended to the rural poor to improve their housing under the Minimum Needs Programme (MNP). Though 627.1 million people live in the villages of India, the housing backlog in this sector is estimated to be 20.6 million.

The Indira Awas Yojana (IAY), a subsidized housing scheme, utilizes 6 per cent of JRY's resources to develop a viable micro-habit, provide housing and ensure a base for higher level or earning for the beneficiaries.

Energy

Other minimum needs such as energy for cooking, heating and lighting by the economically weaker sections are looked after by the Integrated Rural Energy Planning (IREP) which also take care of energy requirement for sustainable agriculture and rural development by providing a cost-effective mix of energy sources. Modified now as a scheme under the Eighth Plan, the IREP was initially started under the Seventh Plan. But the old story of the wide gap between planning and implementaion thwarting any worthwhile progress recurs. The co-ordination between the various sources of energy supply and user agencies was found to be inadequate and suitable extension mechanism at the grass-root level was not available. In India, even we do not have a proper database regarding the energy consumption pattern especially in the rural areas at micro level and the differences in energy use among the villages in terms of different regional characteristics over a period of time. The energy use pattern in Indian villages is greatly influenced by the type and extent of forest cover access, availability of common lands, proximity to urban areas, density of population, agrarian pattern and local tradition.

The first and foremost requirement of rural energy planning in the knowledge about the "ground level realities" of the rural energy scenario such as the present pattern and level of energy use, its determinants, the potential sources of supply for fuels and availability and the inherent problems eventually faced by the rural households in fulfilling their energy requirements.

The present need is for a flexible energy policy which takes into account both short and long term objectives aiming at integration at all level. It is a fact that all the other policies will work well in the rural areas provided the energy policy works well. So, one cannot ignore a suitable energy policy.

Non-conventional energy sources have also emerged as a viable sector for meeting rural energy needs. Around 19 lakh families meet their energy demands from installed bio-gas plants and about 180 lakh household have adopted improved **chullahs**. It is a growing sector with the potential of it transforming the rural energy and environment sense if followed up in right earnest. Only few states like Andhra Pradesh, Gujarat, Haryana, Himachal Pradesh, Karnataka, Kerala, Maharashtra and Punjab have achieved, 100 per cent rural electrification, while states like Bihar and Orissa lag behind with a meager 69.9 per cent and 68.9 per cent respectively. Kerala has, moreover, earned the unique distinction of providing telephone facility to all its 982 village panchayats.

In UP Non Conventional Energy Agency (NCEA) is doing well towards the rural development programme by providing better and improved chullahs and solar cookers. During the present financial year it has distributed 45,000 solar cookers. It has also distributed 500 solar photo voltaic lamps and 3,000 home lightening systems in the rural masses. It's future programmes are to install solar water heaters with the capacity of 50,000 lit./day and to generate nearly 8000 kl. wt. energy through Aero-generators in the hill regions. It has also planned to distribute 73,700 fixed chullahs and 1,36,430 movable chullahs during the financial year 1994-95. Drinking water is a basic human need and providing adequate qualities of safe and clean drinking water for all communities is the primary aim of any water supply scheme. It has been stated that "the number of successfully functioning tube-well, hand-pumps and piped water supply schemes are better indicators of health than the number of hospital beds of doctors". Improving rural water supplies may be on essential step in the development of villages and home industries like fish processing, fruit production, choir making, kitchen gardening, livestock etc. This can increase the productivity of the villages by decreasing the amount of time and energy involved in daily collection of water and in turn will result in better health. Due to adequate water supply and sanitation, villagers' migration to already over crowded cities can also be checked.

Since independence during the period of more than four decades, investment worth more than Rs. 7,000 crores has been made on rural water supply by government has not achieved the required thank till date. To provide safe drinking water to rural population. Water Decade programme was launched in India on 1st April, 1981 to achieve definition targets of coverage of population by 31st March 1991. In order to accelerate this process of providing one of the basic needs of the rural masses. National drinking water mission was also launched as one of the fine societal mission in 1986.

Taking note of on increasing concern about water resource management, the Food and Agricultural Organization (FAO) has selected "Water for life" as the theme of the year 1994 on world food day. Water availability on the globe is limited and cannot be increased by man-made measures. It is, therefore, extremely necessary to harvest this water effectively and to use it efficiently. At present about 60 per cent water in irrigation and otherwise is wasted; this needs to be reduced.

The Central Water Commission has just prepared a draft irrigation and water management strategy within the general framework of National Water Policy. The policy draft has already been approved by the light-powered national water board and is awaiting Cabinet okay. The main objective of the new draft policy is the rationalization of water resources for maximizing agricultural production towards this objective. The policy document envisages that the lower distribution systems of canals, lake distributaries and minors, be handed over to farmers, cooperative organizations for operation and maintenance in a planned manner. It also calls for a restructuring of the government agencies like the irrigation departments and imparting to them an interdisciplinary or multifunctional character.

The new Irrigation Policy aims at achieving the ultimate irrigation potential of 113.5 million hectars by involving the farmer in various aspects of water management. Till 1990-91, only 82.8 million hectars were potentially covered. While UP has performed well to over 24 million hectars out of its ultimate irrigation potential of 25.7 million hectars, of only 4.7 million hectors of irrigated area out of a total potential of 0.2 million hectars.

Information System

Continuous planning requires a systematic management information system for the effective monitoring and evaluation of plan programmes and for imparting necessary flexibility to the planning process. In India, computers have been installed in 80 per cent of the 442 District Rural Development Agencies for this purpose.

The pattern of development therefore can be observed as highly erratic and uneven though rural development receives top priority in government planning. State-wise performances lack uniformity with few states outshining the rest in development, and likewise the successes are overshadowed by abounding failures. The government has hiked the provision for rural development to Rs. 30,000 crore in the Eighth Plan, three times the actual expenditure in the Seventh Plan. But unless the increasing gap between planning and implementation is bridged, all policies, plans and expenditure will be of little help in serving their primary purpose of enriching the real India.

The complex nature of the development problems in the rural areas demand a multi-disciplinary, multi-sectoral and multi-agency approach to rural development planning. A single sectoral approach based on increasing agricultural productivity is not an effective solution to rural backwardness. Poverty cuts across sectors and regions. It arises not only out of reduced agricultural productivity, but also out of unequal distribution. Decentralization of the planning mechanism and people's participation in the formulation and implementation of programmes intended for their benefit are essential for the success of rural development plans.